A Day Like Any Other

All American Tales

A Day Like Any Other

All American Tales

Tim Shea

Published by First Church of Metaphor

FC of M

Copyright © 2015 by Tim Shea
ISBN-13: 978-0692547755
ISBN-10: 0692547754
Edited by Laura K. Deal
Cover photo by Maria Shea
Photoshop and Cover Design by Anna-Maria Crum
Book Design by Anna-Maria Crum
www.FirstChurchofMetaphor.org
Except for public figures, names of the living have
either been used with permission or changed to protect
people's privacy. The tales, like all tales, may have grown
in the telling.

Dedication

▼ ◄ ▲ ▼ ◄ ▲ ▼ ◄ ▲ ▼ ◄ ▲ ▼ ◄ ▲ ▼ ◄ ▲ ▼ ◄ ▲

To my boys, TJ and Nicholas

There has not been a single day in my life that wasn't made better just by you being in it.

I love you more than you'll ever know.

▼ ◄ ▲ ▼ ◄ ▲ ▼ ◄ ▲ ▼ ◄ ▲ ▼ ◄ ▲ ▼ ◄ ▲ ▼ ◄ ▲

Table of Contents

▼◂▲▼◂▲▼◂▲▼◂▲▼◂▲▼◂▲▼◂▲

Foreword

I met Tim in 1972, when our two elementary schools fed us into the same junior high and we both landed as seventh graders in orchestra. Tim played bass. I played viola. For the next six years, we shared that community of the school orchestra, though our worlds didn't overlap beyond that. Tim, a gifted athlete, played football, wrestled, lifted weights; I, with no athletic bent at all, focused on the fantasy worlds I found in books and the ones I created in my own head. Both of us were too reserved to bridge the gap.

Our paths parted after we graduated from high school and we lost touch. Tim went into coaching for a while. I went on to grad school. We created families, and our paths didn't cross again until we bumped into each other on Facebook when our class planned our 30th reunion.

I don't remember now which one of us reached out with that friend request, but it doesn't matter. Turns out, each of us likes hanging on to friendships, and our shared experience of orchestra, stilted though it was by adolescent social structures, was enough of a foundation for us to build a more comfortable, mature friendship. Reading Tim's Facebook posts, I discovered what I wish I had known in my teen years. Tim is funny, and a great storyteller, with a deep respect for other humans and a compassionate heart.

In the summer of 2013, I published my first book, just in time to have it debut at the Waking the Dreamer Within Festival, which I had helped organize. The steep learning curve and short publishing time-frame compressed a lot of stress into the process. In the final throes of birthing that project, I vowed I would never, ever, do it again. Then I read another of Tim's posts and knew, without doubt, that I wanted to see his stories out in the world in book form.

I didn't say anything. I was busy.

The day after I returned from the Festival, Tim contacted me about a dream a friend of his had told him about, and asked if I had any projections:

> I had leopard tattoos on my forearms—from my wrist to my elbows. It looked amazing! Later in the dream I looked down at my arms and said, "What have I done!"

As I read the dream, the tingle of an "aha" ran down my arms. I told Tim:

> At the dream portrayal workshop this weekend, the dreamer picked a long leopard-print cloth to represent a symbol in her dream. Projections that arose in that work focused on wild energies that I (the dreamer) am figuring out how to work with.

The synchronicity of leopard tattoos and leopard cloth showing up so close in time affirmed for me that this event was part of a larger pattern, and I should pay attention. My projections on the dream continued:

> Wrist to elbow is way cool, in my imagined version of this dream, because it's the area of the body that supports and facilitates my use of my hands, and hands are how I do my work in the world/express myself on FB/manipulate my environment. So this dream, for me, is a celebration of how I've been able to channel these wild energies to help me manifest the world

I live in.

I love the paradox of knowing how beautiful these markings are and also the alarm of, "What have I done?" From my own marking dreams, I've come to see that when I really see a truth about myself (leopard tattoos), there's no going back. My tattoos are permanent. Also "forearm" makes me think of "forefathers" and I wonder what work I'm doing in the world to help heal ancestral patterns in my life....

I couldn't ignore what the act of imagining the leopard print tattoos awoke in me. I'd been thinking about Tim's book of essays, and knew that I had to use my hands to help it manifest. I knew that this act of creation would leave metaphorical marks on me; the book itself would be etched into my heart as well as part of my identity in the world. And, it would be a work that would help keep the ancestors alive in the most human way we can—through stories.

I sent Tim another message, right on the heels of my projections on the dream:

Even when I was in the depths of determination to never, ever, go through publishing a book again, your stories awoke this longing to see the collection published in the world. So much that I want to get in the first bid on your book.

Your post about the Eagle today resonated with a powerful moment at the Festival, when one of the few men in attendance pulled an eagle card from a deck and had such an 'aha' that he stood there in tears for a while.

Eagle, for me, is about seeing the big picture and yet being able to dive in and strike when warranted.

You've got that gift when you tell stories, Tim. Setting the stage and getting into the heart in what...a couple hundred words? It's a gift, and I'd love to be on the team that makes a book out of it. And that's God's honest truth. Think about it. And meanwhile, copy those posts into a Word file!

Wisely, Tim didn't commit to anything right away, suggesting that we talk on the phone soon. But he did sign off with, "I might possibly just send you what I have and let you do with it as you will."

As you can see, eventually he did, and I know the world is richer for it.

And to Tim, thanks for trusting me. It's been an honor to play my part in this unusual duet of ours.

—Laura K. Deal

Author's Preface

In 2006, my life took some unwelcome turns, started bucking uncontrollably, and eventually threw me. When I landed, I landed hard, and found myself in an unfamiliar and very unsettling place. Within a period of about three years, I had lost my career of 17 years, my marriage, my self-respect, and my internal compass. I couldn't make sense of any of it, and I was in a lot of pain.

In the summer of 2009, still struggling, I made the decision to attend my high school class reunion. I had never been to a reunion before, and most rational people would have avoided that one at all costs. But for some reason, I felt like I needed to go, so I did. And it changed my life.

I had never written anything before, unless it was assigned in school, but when I returned home, I was so moved by the experience, that I had to find a way to get it out. I can't write music and talking about it with friends just wasn't enough. So one day, I sat down at my computer and just started writing.

I wrote about how being around people who only knew the 18-year-old kid from 30 years ago gave me some hope that the kid might still be alive somewhere inside of me, and that just maybe I could find him again.

When I finished writing it up, I took a chance and shared it with a friend. And it made her cry. Then I shared it with another friend, and it made her cry. And then I shared it with a few others, and they all told me to keep writing. I didn't know why, because it was just 'that one thing' and it wasn't good anyway.

A year or so later, I made a short road trip and decided that I would make some notes while I was on the road and just play with it. I shared some of what I had seen and where I had been, and people told me to keep writing.

After a couple of years of this, my dear friend, Laura K. Deal—a real writer—told me that she wanted to put some of my stuff together and publish it. After I stopped laughing, I asked her what she had in mind, and she told me, "Just send me what you have, and keep going. I'll do the rest." I really thought she had slipped a gear, but I figured that I would humor her. Little did I know, she was not looking to be humored. She was serious, and she knew what she was doing. I am still, however, not sure why she took a chance on me, but I am eternally grateful that she did.

I certainly haven't figured everything out, but I do know this; the only thing I have ever done in my life that didn't have a goal attached to it, is write stories. Writing stories, talking about people I've met or things that I've seen, is the only thing I've ever done in my life purely for the pleasure of doing it.

There is no way that I could ever mention all of the people who gently, (and not so gently), prodded me to put these stories together. I can only say that they believed in it far more than I ever did. So to my little playgroup, I want to offer a humble and sincere thank you. You know who you are and you know that I love you. Every last one of you.

Contained in these pages are the observations, happenstances, and random conversations that I've had over the past few years, with friends, family, and perfect strangers. Things that seemed to drop into my lap, at no special time and in no particularly special way. Things that happened on a day like any other.

Learning the Game

▶▼▲▶▼▲▶▼▲▶▼▲

▲ ▶ ▼ ▲ ▶ ▼ ▲ ▶ ▼ ▲ ▶ ▼ ▲ ▶ ▼ ▲ ▶ *Little Cleats*

I drove over to Charlestown last night and donated a pair of good condition, used football cleats to the youth football program there. I had been away from that program for a few years, but I coached there for four years and still feel an attachment to it. The program is mostly comprised of kids from the projects in Charlestown. Kids who live lives that most of us can't imagine.

My first year in the program, my fullback had anger management issues, my quarterback had emotional issues, and my tailback used to come to practice so hungry that he couldn't pay attention because he hadn't eaten all day. His mother was an addict, his father was long gone, and many nights this kid would sleep on his living room floor because somebody he didn't know would be passed out on his bed.

Many nights, after practice, our program director would shut off the lights and head to his car to find this kid and his little brother standing there waiting for him. They wouldn't say anything to him when he got there.

They would just stand there looking down. He also grew up in those projects and he knew what was going on. He would say hi and ask them how their day was. They offered little to nothing in return. Then he would ask them if they had eaten today. They would just shake their heads, still not looking up at him. So he would tell them to get in the car and he would take the kid and his little brother to get something to eat before sending them home. (I didn't even know about it until the season was over.)

I had a defensive back who showed up at every practice and really seemed to enjoy it, but he never made it to the games. When I asked one of his friends why he didn't come, he said, "'Cuz he be playin' basketball till two o'clock in the morning, then he can't get up."

"His parents let him play basketball till two in the morning?!"

The kid said, "His mama don't know where he at. She don't care nothin' about him."

He was eight years old.

My left guard was trying to deal with the fact that his father was literally on his death bed from cancer. His father never saw him play and passed just after the season ended.

One of my kids missed a couple of days of practice in a row, which was unlike him. When I asked him about it he explained to me that he had to stay home and translate for his mom when the men in the suits came by to talk to her.

These kids weren't easy to coach, because most every adult they had ever known had either betrayed them or left them. Adults couldn't be trusted. They learned to fight back at a very young age. Our first practice looked like something out of "The Longest Yard." The first time they hit each other, I had to break up three fights. They didn't know football. They only knew fighting and survival. It was a long season. But one of the things that I will always remember about that season was our touchdown. Our ONE touchdown.

On a designed sweep, one of our kids broke free around the left end and took it to the house. It wasn't called back, and we got all six points. As I remember, it was a pretty long run too. You would have thought we had just won the league championship. Kids were hugging each other on the sidelines. Coaches were hugging kids and coaches were hugging each other. The few parents that showed up at the game were screaming in the stands and jumping up and down. I even caught one of the referees smiling. But most of all—the kids, those sweet kids, were cheering and laughing. All of them. One of the coaches even had to wipe away tears. I won't say which one.

That was seven years ago. Seven long years ago. Seven short years ago. The kids on that team have long since outgrown the program and are on to other things. Now it's populated with a new bunch from the same projects. A new bunch of kids dealing with the same issues that mine did.

It all came back to me yesterday when I walked across that empty field to donate a used pair of cleats to be given to a kid who can't afford them. Here's hoping that they'll be put to good use. That they might even help some kid get around the left end and take it all the way in for a touchdown. Here's hoping that in some small way, they might help to bring smiles and laughter to every kid on the team, and maybe even a tear to a coach's eye.

▼▲ ▶▼▲ ▶▼▲ ▶▼▲ ▶▼▲ ▶▼▲ ▶▼▲ ▶ *ABC's*

I just walked down to my local laundromat and was met at the door by a two- or three-year-old girl carrying one of those little computer toys with the little ducky on the top that sings the alphabet song. She was playing with it and was singing along until her eyes caught mine. Beautiful, stunning, dark brown eyes. As I sometimes frighten small children, I smiled at her and said, "You are a really good singer!" and then just looked away and kept walking.

A few seconds after I got to my dryer, I felt a sharp tug on my left pant leg. I looked down to find this little girl standing right beside me and holding her little computer in her hand. She cranked it up, and started singing again. "aaaaa beeee CEEEE DEEEEE EEEEEE...."

So I gave her a little more this time. "Mija! Where did you learn to sing like that? You're really good!!" and I thought that that would be the end of it. But about then I noticed her grandmother looking at me and thought, "Oh great, here's where they call the police."

Fortunately, however, she was smiling at me, and she said with a thick accent, "She want you to sing with her."

I paused for a moment and then said, "You're kidding...."

She shook her head no, and kept smiling.

Well, now I'm in it.

So I turned back to the little girl and said, "Will you help me with the tough parts? I'm not sure I know all the words." She looked up at me and nodded her head and then hit the button. I squatted down to her level and off we went. I mean, if you're gonna do it, do it right. Right?

"aaaaa beeee CEEEE DEEEE EEEEEE....," and then I threw in a T where it didn't belong. She looked surprised, stared at me for a couple of seconds, and then she just shook her head. What I did NOT count on, is that the little machine didn't pick up where it left off. Oh no. It went all the way back to the beginning. So she hit the button and off we went again. This time, for fun, I threw in a K at some random place. Now she was onto me. She broke into this huge smile and started laughing. Two-year-old laughter is Kryptonite to me. I have no defenses whatsoever. I was toast.

So she started us over...again...and off we went. This went on for about 15 or 20 minutes; me screwing it up, her squealing, and me melting. After what seemed like a few hundred rounds, she went to her Grandmother, pointed at me and said, "He disn't know the awfulbet."

Well, the kid brought the house down. I roared, Nana laughed, the two ladies on the other side of the folding tables laughed, and the lady changing money behind the counter laughed. Apparently, we had built quite an audience in that place. I didn't notice them because I couldn't take my eyes off of her, and if she noticed them, she clearly didn't care.

After we wrapped up our little game and I had put my things together, I stopped to thank that baby for letting me play. I told her that I would practice until I saw her again and that next time I would do better. She just said, "OK," and gave me one of those little grins where you can see the baby teeth and the dimples. Yeah...that one. So I headed out the door with a smile on my face and thought, "That was the absolute perfect ending to this day."

▶▼▲ ▶▼▲ ▶▼▲ ▶▼▲ ▶▼▲ ▶▼▲ ▶ *All-Stars*

Last night my ten year old, Nick, played in his first All-Star baseball game. Overall he played well and his team won by two or three runs. On the way home after the game, Nick, his brother, TJ, and I had a great time talking about the game and some of the plays made by both teams. TJ threw in a couple of memories from the All-Star game that he played in last year, but he wasn't being competitive. Actually, quite the opposite. He was adding to Nick's story and validating Nick's experience as only a big brother can. It was really a great ride home. I told Nick how proud I was of him for making the team and told him that I hoped that above all, he had fun. Through the "perma-grin" on his face, he said that he did and that he wanted to do it again.

When we got home and pulled into the garage, TJ hopped out of the back seat and Nick opened his door to exit the "Seat of Honor" (i.e. shotgun).

TJ said, "Nick, let's go play that new game we got!"

And Nick said, "OK, but first I have to put this away."

Then Nick walked around the front of the car to a shelf in the garage where TJ's All-Star hat from last year was sitting. Nick gently moved it to one side and then took off his hat and set it down next to TJ's. Then he bolted up the stairs after his brother.

I told them that I'd be up in a minute. For that minute, or whatever it was, I stood in front of the shelf and looked at those two little hats, side by side. As I stood there, I'll bet a thousand memories washed over me, one after the other. The first time I ever rolled a little plastic ball across the floor to them. The first time I taught them to throw and catch a ball. The first practice in Tee Ball. The first time they ever made a catch in a game, or got a hit. I even remember the games, one for each of them, where they played catcher and threw four base runners out who were attempting to steal second or third base.

I also remember walking out to the pitcher's mound on a few occasions to calm one of them down and give him a chance to dry the tears that were welling up in his eyes as he was getting shelled, with no defensive help whatsoever. Most times I could make them laugh at the situation, at least a little, but sometimes even my best stuff wasn't enough.

I was proud of the "All Star" labels on those hats, but it didn't begin to compare with the pride and profound sense of gratitude I was feeling about the boys who had worn them.

▲ ▷ ▼ ▲ ▷ ▼ ▲ ▷ ▼ ▲ ▷ ▼ ▲ ▷ ▼ ▲ ▷ ▼ ▲ ▷ *Dreams*

I punched in at 4:00 a.m. for an overtime shift today and I had the pleasure of working with an 18-year-old kid whom I had never met before. I chatted him up for a while and learned that he had dropped out of high school, gotten his G.E.D., and had been working two jobs for meager wages ever since. He was glad to be working for a good company with a good reputation, but as we talked while we worked, he started to open up a bit.

He said, "I can't really believe that this is all there is, ya know? I mean, were we really meant to just get up and work our asses off every day our whole lives at something we don't really like, just to keep food on the table?" I just kinda let him go—I wanted to see where it went.

I asked him, "What would you be doing if money were no object? I mean, if every job paid exactly the same, and it was all enough to live on comfortably."

"Well, I don't really want to say. You'll just laugh."

"Try me."

"All right. I'm a dancer. I like to dance."

"No kidding? What kind do you do?"

"You ever heard of 'Poppin'??"

"Sure. I can't do it, but I know about it."

"I'm honestly good at it. And I take it seriously. I mean, I'm always learning, and I love to teach it. If I could make a living doing that, I'd be happy forever. But I guess in this world, you can't always do what you want."

This boy opened exactly the wrong door to exactly the wrong person. The kinder, gentler Tim got mugged, and the coach suddenly stepped up. Nobody invited him, mind you, least of all, the kid, but he showed up anyway.

"How old did you say you are?"

"Eighteen."

"DUDE, YOU HAVEN'T EVEN GOTTEN OUTTA THE GATE YET!!! YOU'RE STILL A KID!! DON'T YOU DARE LET ME HEAR YOU TALK ABOUT PUTTING DREAMS AWAY AT YOUR AGE!!! NOW IS WHEN YOU START WORKING TO MAKE 'EM HAPPEN!!!! THIS IS THE STARTING LINE!!! YOU CAN'T EVEN SEE THE FINISH LINE FROM HERE!!! ARE YOU KIDDIN' ME?!!!"

And on it went. And on...and on. "DO YOU KNOW WHAT I WAS DOING AT YOUR AGE??" He didn't care, but I told him anyway. "IF I HAD LISTENED TO EVERYBODY WHO TOLD ME I COULDN'T...."

"Yeah!!! That's what I keep getting!! Nobody believes in me!"

"Buddy, you're gonna hear that all your life!! Forget 'em! The people who are the best at telling you that you can't do something are the very same people that aren't doing anything! You understand?!"

"Yeah. Ya know, I just read a book called *The Secret*. Have you ever heard of it?"

"Sure."

"Do you think that stuff is true?"

"I think it's based in truth. I think that the more you focus on something the more your life will move in that direction—whatever it is, good or bad. But here's the thing—you just essentially told me that you are already losing focus. YOU CAN'T DO THAT! NOW IS WHEN YOU HAVE TO FOCUS HARDER THAN YOU'VE EVER FOCUSED BE-FORE!!"

OK—now this kid is startin' to feel me. And it's a good thing, 'cuz I'm working myself into a lather. "Listen, I don't know anything about dancing, unless it's the Texas two-step—and I don't know a whole lot about that."

"The what...?"

"Never mind. I want your phone number and I want your email address before we leave here today. I know people who know people and sometimes it's just about catchin' a break."

"Aw, man, you would help me?"

"Pardner, I've had a lot of dreams in my life. I made some of them happen, and I fell on my face with others, but I was never afraid to take a shot. When it comes to somebody with a dream—I mean a real dream, I turn into a wildcat. Are you willing to move?"

"I'll go anywhere."

"Are you willing to put in a lot of hours perfecting what you do? Are you willing to network?"

"I already practice all the time, but I don't know much about networking."

"Well I do. I learned it from coaching. Don't worry about it. We're gonna find a way."

"Man, I can't believe this. If I could just...."

"Also, take 'just' out of your vocabulary. I don't want to hear it again. I want you to start seeing where you want to be, and nothing else. Focus on it. Get it into the front of your mind. Stop qualifying."

"OK. So you know about poppin' and hip-hop and everything?"

"How old do you think I am?"

"Well, no disrespect, but you gotta be at least as old as my mom."

"OK. How old is your mom?"

"Well, again, no disrespect—she's like...41."

"Forty-one.... Yeah, I passed 41 a few exits back. But, I do know what you're talkin' about. Look—this isn't about what your dream is. This is about that you don't stop dreaming. Not ever."

"Yeah.... I think I get it. You really think I could do this?"

"The question is—do YOU think you can do this?"

"Yeah. I actually think that maybe I could."

"Good. For now, that's all we need. Now let's get this can buttoned up and loaded."

Then as quickly as he came, the coach went back to wherever he hibernates and Tim showed back up. I slapped the kid on the shoulder and said, "I'll see ya tomorrow morning."

"Hey Tim—thanks, man."

"Nah, man. Thank you."

▼▲ ▶▼▲ ▶▼▲ ▶▼▲ ▶▼▲ ▶▼▲ ▶ *Bittersweet*

On my way home from work tonight, I had the pleasure of one of those bittersweet moments we all occasionally get. As I was stopped at a traffic light, I looked off
to my right and saw a Little League baseball field with
a bunch of kids on it who couldn't have been a day over
six or seven years old, dressed in shirts, hats, and wearing
ball gloves, all of which were two sizes too big. The sight
of it gave me a little tug and as I wasn't in a huge hurry
to get home, I pulled into the parking lot and just sat and
watched for a few minutes.

As they were trying to play catch, I found myself drawn
to a lot of the things that I missed as a coach and even as a
young dad. The things that you spend hours and days trying to correct if you're building the All-Stars of tomorrow.
Their mechanics were awful. Their throwing motions were
all wrong, their gloves were pointing the wrong way when
they attempted to catch, and they weren't set to catch the
ball once it was thrown to them.

But tonight it was different. Granted, it wasn't my team,
but I honestly think that had they been, I still wouldn't

have cared. Not now. Not tonight. And I shouldn't have cared as much ten years ago when my guys were the same ages. I was never harsh with any of my kids. I was always in it for the fun. Both their fun and my fun. But at the same time, I was trying to teach. I was trying to teach technique, fundamentals, rules, sportsmanship and once in a great while, even a little strategy, just to keep it interesting. But it dawned on me tonight that I may have missed some things. Maybe a lot of things.

As I watched the kids practice, I noticed their official team T-shirts which hung down past their knees. I noticed their oversized hats which were pulled down to the bridges of their noses. I noticed their oversized gloves, and their little cleats, and the water bottles on the bench, and the kid in the field by himself who was down on his hands and knees looking intently into the grass. I assumed he had seen a bug that he had to get another look at. I noticed the smiles and the squeals and how they all jumped when one of them would throw the ball and then the whole pack would chase after it to see who could get there first.

As I watched these kids, I was reminded of my boys at the same ages. I remembered my oldest who was facing a pitcher four years older than he was and throwing gas. I mean I have never seen a 12- year-old kid throw a ball that hard. My son was 0-2 in the count, and as he stepped out of the box after a called second strike, he looked over to the bench and yelled, "Johnny! Don't eat all the Starbursts!"

I remembered my youngest going down on three consecutive called strikes. When I asked him why he didn't swing he told me, "By the time my brain tells my arms to swing, the ball is already past me."

I have a thousand memories of my guys playing ball. Memories of strike-outs, missed grounders, and some bad throws here and there. I also remember both of my boys playing catcher and throwing kids out who were attempting to steal second or third base. I remember them cheering their teammates on from the dugout and taking a victory lap around the bases after a win. And I remember the laughing, the smiles, the horseplay, and trying to find gloves and hats when it was time to go home.

I think that on some level I even knew at the time that those memories would stay with me, but I didn't know what they would feel like all these years later. I didn't realize that the memories would leave an empty longing to do it all again. But this time to really take it all in as it was happening. To not miss a thing. Not one thing.

I would do it all again in a heartbeat. Teaching my guys how to throw, how to hold their gloves and "Don't stab at the ball—let it come to you." How to shorten their swing, "chop the tree," "throw your hands at it," "turn your hips," and a hundred other little things. In looking back at it, I hope that they never got the wrong idea about what I was trying to do then. I hope that they still know, all these years later, that the games were never the most important thing to me. The games were incidental. I honestly don't remember the details or the scores of any of them. I only remember watching my guys play, in their oversized hats and gloves and jerseys hanging down to their knees. And how much I wish I could do it all again.

▲ ▷ ▼ ▲ ▷ ▼ ▲ ▷ ▼ ▲ ▷ ▼ ▲ ▷ ▼ ▲ ▷ *Coach Buck*

"That kid couldn't hit a bull in the butt with a banjo...."

"What...?"

"Weren't you talking about the quarterback?"

"Yeah. I said, if he timed it right, he could have hit the Y on the seam route."

"We're not recruiting him. He can't throw."

"He's got a pretty strong arm, Coach."

"Yeah, but he can't get it in the right zip code!"

And so went the film session, like so many others, with one of funniest and most colorful characters I have ever met in my life. I had the privilege of coaching football for a year at the University of Northern Colorado, back in 1985, and a man by the name of Buck Rollins was the defensive backs coach on that staff. He had been there since I was in the first grade, and would be there for years after I had left. He had a great sense of the line between work and play, coaching and teaching, praise and reprimand, and even in the middle of a good butt chewing, his position guys would gather around him, listen intently, and laugh all the way through it. His guys loved playing for him, and they always gave him everything they had.

Buck was born in Lamar, Colorado in 1932, which, particularly then, was nothing but wide open prairie and farm land as far as the eye could see. I asked him what growing up out there was like then and he said, "Well, f*#kin', fightin' and freight train ridin' was all there was to do, so that's pretty much all we did."

He played football at Colorado State University, and then went into coaching at UNC in 1967, so he was an older coach by the time I got there. He coached on a lot of bad teams (including the team the year that I was there), and he also coached some really good ones. But good or bad, Buck was always Buck. He had the ability to turn a phrase, and you always paid attention to what he was saying, partly because you didn't want to miss one of his nuggets, and partly because he was almost always right.

One time in a staff meeting, our head coach asked him about a variation to a pass coverage he wanted to use that week. Buck said, "Coach, right now our pass defense is to watch the ball sail over our heads and then run as fast as we can to catch up. So, sure—let's try anything."

When our head coach asked him about having one of our linebackers make some defensive adjustments on the fly, Buck said, "Coach, the kid couldn't figure out how to pour water out of a boot if you wrote the instructions on the heel. He can't do that."

During a staff meeting in the middle of the summer two-a-day practices, one of our coaches mentioned the name of a coach on another staff. Buck kind of rolled his eyes and said, "I know that guy. He couldn't coach ducks to water."

In preparation for an opponent who ran the triple option to near perfection, our head coach decided that our best chance at stopping them was to cover everybody but the quarterback, and make him run the ball on every play until he got too tired to be effective. (The rest of us, including Buck, knew it was going to be a disaster—and it was.) On hearing this new plan, he muttered under his breath, "Yeah, maybe we'll get lucky and the kid will have a heart attack."

During that same film session, the film projector had come slightly out of focus, but our head coach didn't seem to notice it. After a couple of minutes, Buck finally piped up in that low, slow drawl of his, and said, "Coach...either I'm havin' a stroke or that projector is out of focus."

And on it went. When the other position players were running out of gas in practice, Buck's guys always seemed to have energy. For some reason, when every other guy on the field had his head down and was gasping for breath, Buck's guys had their heads up—and they were always laughing. Even during practice.

I haven't even scratched the surface of the things that would come out of his mouth, but you get the idea. This was a funny but disciplined football coach, who not only loved football, but loved coaching college kids. Actually, I think he just loved kids. Football was a way to be around them.

After one particularly tough defeat in Iowa, I walked into a small room just off of the locker room where Buck was sitting, and he was clearly dejected and tired. I was too. Our eyes met, but neither one of us said anything. He looked down for a minute and then looked back at me and said, "This is a helluva way to make a livin' ain't it?" And actually, it really was.

I found out last week that Buck died after a long battle with cancer. I thought about him a lot this past week. I thought about the work we put in and the disappointment of that season. But mostly I thought about how much fun he was. You may have had to know him and be around him a while to really get it, but he was one of those rare birds who really leaves an impression. His players, to a man, loved him and loved playing for him. His fellow coaches loved him, and as far as I know, just about everybody who ever met him loved him.

I hope that there's a special place for him in the Great Beyond, where he is relaxed and enjoying himself as much as he did here. I hope that he is surrounded by family and friends and a whole bunch of people who didn't get to know him here. I hope he's telling stories again with that dry, monotone wit of his, because if he is, you can guarantee that there will be a group gathered around him, listening intently and laughing until their sides hurt.

Rest in peace, Buck. It was a real pleasure knowing you and coaching with you.

▶▼▲▶ Ultimate Fighting Championship

So tonight the boys were going all UFC up in the bedroom while I was downstairs trying to get a little work done. I could tell from the noise I was hearing and from the tiny pieces of plaster that were falling from the ceiling, directly below the "ring," that they had a good match going.

At some point in the match, I'm guessing in about the third round, I had to enter the room to put some things away, but I was stopped in my tracks because the door would only open a crack.

I said, "Guys, make a hole, I gotta get in."

So do you think they stopped the match and then got up and moved? If you do, you don't have teenage boys. Or maybe you just don't have teenage boys who are prone to move the beds to clear out a space to hone their wrestling and fighting skills on one another.

What they did—with TJ pinning Nick to his back, and with Nick holding TJ in some kind of a reverse headlock death grip—is just scooch across the floor, together, without either one releasing the grip that he had on the other, and then ask, "Is that enough room?"

I said, "Yeah, that'll do...."

And then they went right back at it.

I put my stuff away and said, "Let me know how it comes out."

I remembered my brother and me doing the same thing at the same age, and I couldn't help smiling a little as I walked back out the door.

▶▼▲ ▶▼▲ ▶▼▲ ▶▼▲ ▶▼▲ ▶▼▲ ▶ *Swimmers*

When I was in college, I majored in Education: specifically, Physical Education. One of the most impactful requirements made on me by my program was to gain teaching experience by teaching a group of rowdy second graders to swim. The elementary school nearest our university had always had a great, collegial relationship with the university, so when our program directors called their principal to ask if they would mind bringing the second graders over for yet another year of lessons, they were happy to oblige.

I very much enjoyed teaching these kids. Some of them could swim like dolphins, and some of them were afraid of the water. For reasons unknown to me, we didn't split the kids up by skill level. It was a random draw, and each of us "instructors" got five or six kids with whom to work. The kids who could already swim, or who even had an idea about it, made you look like a better teacher. You wanted at least a few of them in your group so that it looked like you knew what you were doing.

That being said, my favorites were the kids who were afraid of the water. The kids who not only didn't know how to swim, but didn't trust us to teach them. In fact, didn't trust anything. Not the instructors, the pool, the building, the water...none of it. These kids, upon being instructed to put their faces in the water, would try to convince me that they had already done it but that I just hadn't seen them do it. This, of course, can happen if you're not paying close attention. In fact, according to them, it happened every time I asked them to do it. I thought it odd that neither their faces nor hair were wet, but I let it go.

I remember lining my guys up on the side of the pool, feet in the water, and talking to them about what we would be doing, how we would do it, and why none of them had to be afraid. I let them know that I was a strong swimmer and that I had never lost a kid in the pool, and I wasn't going to start with one of them. They didn't care. Most of them were just over three feet tall, and they could tell by looking that the water in the pool was deeper than that. That meant that there was more water in the pool than they had inches in height, and that, in turn, was bad news.

But, somehow, we got through that first day and as the days went by, things got a little better and my guys began to trust me. I mean, why wouldn't they? I really hadn't asked much of them to this point. I hadn't given them any reason *not* to trust me. All good, right? Well, it was, right up until I revealed my whole purpose for having them in there. My intention wasn't just to allow them some fun time to splash around in the shallow end of the pool. My intention was to teach them to swim. In deep water. That was the whole point of the lessons, and I think that on some level they knew that before they got there. But the reality of the situation hits home when an instructor actually takes you to the deep water and says, "HERE is where we will be working for the rest of the time."

The day that I moved my little group of ducklings to the "deep end of the pool" was an anxiety-ridden day, to put it mildly. I, of course, was fine. I was in control. I knew how to swim, and I knew that I could take any kid who came my way, and lead him back to safety. It simply was not a problem. The kids, however, had their doubts. They didn't trust me anymore. Forgetting that I had never yet let them down, and that I was still in control, they went back to their fears. They certainly didn't trust themselves, and they didn't trust the ten feet of water that they saw in the pool. Some of the kids got real quiet. Some were visibly shaken, and a few outright cried. But I made sure that every one of them got in that pool with me. The ones who saw it as an adventure and took a shot at swimming did very well. They wanted the adventure. They trusted me not to let them down. The ones who weren't sure, I held onto until they calmed down, and then I would get them close enough to the side of the pool to *almost* reach it—but not quite. I would cut them loose, and then give them a little nudge toward the side of the pool. They always made it, and their eyes would light up once they realized what they had just done all by their little selves.

But my favorites were the ones who were really scared. Crying scared. Need to be helped into the water by another teacher, scared. Those were the kids that I held onto the tightest. They were the ones I kept talking to. The ones I kept telling how well they were swimming and how impressed I was with them. They didn't care. They're the ones who I had to peel off of my neck and just let them hang onto the side of the pool while we talked. Then I would take them out a few feet, and push them back to the wall. Out a few more feet, and push them to the wall. Out a few more feet, and against their staunchest objections, peel them off of my neck and push them toward the wall, not hard enough to get them there, but hard enough to get them moving.

They always had to swim a few strokes on their own, and when they got to the wall, gasping, coughing, sputtering, and with panic in their eyes, just before they could start crying again, I would meet them there with an "I CAN'T BELIEVE WHAT YOU JUST DID!!" (This always stunned them.) I would say, "Stay right here," and then I would swim out to the spot from which they began their swim. I would exclaim, "THIS IS WHERE YOU STARTED! YOU JUST SWAM FROM HERE TO THERE...BY YOURSELF!!"

That did it. At that very moment, they realized that their heartless, uncaring instructor actually did care, and actually was capable of taking them through that horrible deep water. That the deep water was actually no different than the shallow water, and that, above all, they *could* swim. They went from being helped into the water to begging to go off the diving board "Just once more! PLEEEEEEZE?!!!"

Nothing about their circumstances had changed from the time they were scared to death, to the time they were jumping off the diving board and making silly faces on the way down. The only thing that changed was their perception of the water, and, perhaps more importantly, their perception of their instructor. They finally realized that the guy in the pool actually knew what he was doing and wanted to help.

But the very best part of it all was watching what happened in their little spirits when they went from being afraid of the water to conquering their fear. And that's why I made each kid get into that water with me —against his will. That's why I made him swim when he *knew* he couldn't. When they all finished swimming, they weren't scared anymore. They had conquered the water, and moreover, they had conquered their fear. Now they were swimmers.

In thinking back on this time and remembering some of the lessons that I delivered as well as those that I learned, I was struck by a comparison that I hadn't thought of until I started to write this out. How many times has our loving God called us into the deep water, not to scare us or torment us, but simply to show us that He is with us and that we have nothing to fear? How many times has He longed to show us that no matter how deep the water gets, He is still in control and He won't let us slip under? Why does He do this? To make us stronger? To make us braver? To hone our characters to a razor sharp edge, thus making us ready for some heroic service? Maybe.

But I wonder if sometimes He calls us into that deep water just because He loves swimming with us. And He knows that it is while we are still afraid of the deep water, and learning to swim, that we will hold tightest to Him. And maybe...just maybe, our God simply loves the feeling of holding His children.

▷▼▲ ▷▼▲ ▷▼▲ ▷▼▲ ▷▼▲ ▷ *Coach Kenny*

My college roommate, JW Lively, and I both played football for our college team, and we both had a dream to coach football at the college level after we graduated. Most of our classmates and teammates wanted to coach high school football, and in Texas, that is a lofty goal in and of itself. But JW and I were hell bent for leather to coach in college. We had no idea of how we were going to make that happen, but we were young, ambitious, and didn't have sense enough not to try.

One weekend while we were still in college and be-yond broke, we took everything we had out of the bank and registered to attend a football clinic in San Antonio. I called the guy who ran the clinic to be sure that we could still get in. I talked to him for a few minutes, and in as-sessing our situation he asked me if the entrance fee would be a problem for us. I told him that it most definitely was, but that we were not going to let that stop us, and that we would sell pencils on the street corner if we had to, until we came up with the money to get in.

He said, "Come and see me when you get here. I'll help you out." When we got there, we asked for him and he came to the registration table. He told the lady that JW and I were there as his guests and he let us attend free of charge. I've never forgotten him for that.

The keynote speaker at the clinic that weekend was an up-and-coming football coach by the name of Ken Hatfield, who had just finished a coaching stint at the United States Air Force Academy. He was subsequently hired as the head coach of the University of Arkansas, one of the premier football programs in the United States. He had just been voted America's "Coach of the Year," for the job he did at Air Force. His team beat Notre Dame that season. He was a rock star.

JW and I decided that that was who we would work for. Just...decided. So we set out to meet him at the conference. We didn't see him until about 15 minutes before he was to take the stage to deliver his keynote speech in front of a thousand high-school and college football coaches. As he was making his way to the front, amid the back slaps, handshakes and other greetings, we ambushed him. We told him that we HAD to talk to him. That it was of the utmost importance. (It was.) And he very kindly explained that he was about to deliver his speech and then he had to catch a plane right after he was done. A multimillion dollar booster was driving him to the airport right after he finished speaking, so there was no time. We said, "Coach —let US take you to the airport!!"

He said, "Guys, this guy is a big deal down there—I should go with him."

We weren't having it. We said, "Coach, PLEASE! Let us take you! We HAVE to talk to you!"

Do you know what that man did? The Coach of the Year sighed, dropped his head, and said, "All right. I'll tell him that you're taking me. Now, before we do this—do you KNOW where the airport is? I CANNOT miss this flight!"

We said, "Of course we do! We'll get you right there!"

So he said, "OK. Meet me here, right after I'm done." And then he walked away to head up to the stage.

I turned to my buddy, JW, and said, "J...we have exactly one hour to figure out where the airport is." So we found the concierge of the hotel, got directions, went over them several times, rehearsed them, quizzed each other on them, and then decided that we were all set. Kenny delivered a bang up presentation and got a standing ovation.

Right after he finished, JW met Coach Hatfield at the designated spot and I went to the front to have the valet pull my 1978 Plymouth Volare (with real Corinthian leather), around to the front door of the hotel.

Now, what I had forgotten was that JW and I had TRASHED that car from a long road trip out, eating our takeout meals IN IT because we couldn't afford the hotel food. We weren't real particular about what we did with the boxes and wrappers (other than not throwing them out the window), and we hadn't as yet taken the time to find a dumpster. I mean, there was no real hurry, and eventually it would all get thrown out, right? We were still young and other than mapping out our impressive career paths, we didn't really plan for the unforeseeable. Or at least we didn't that weekend. So, when I went to the car and opened the door, I saw something that looked like an episode of Hoarders dead in front of me. In all the excitement of the weekend and particularly what had taken place that day, I had completely forgotten about the car.

The blood drained from my face, and then I started moving. In fact, I don't know that I have ever moved faster in my life. I threw every bag, rapper, container, can, notebook, and whatever else was in there, into the back seat as fast as I could, to clean out a spot in the front seat for...did I mention it yet? The Coach of the Year. So when coach Hatfield got to my car, do you know what he did? He opened the front door, moved the seat lever (two door), and got...into...the...back...seat. At 23 years old, I am sure that I had a heart attack. Right there on that curb. JW had one too.

I yelled, just loud enough to be heard on the River Walk, "COACH! YOU SIT IN THE FRONT!!"

He said, "No, guys I'm fine! This is no problem!" Then he put his suit case on his lap—because there was no room on the seat—and I had my second heart attack. At this point I'm thinking that our chances of being hired have just dropped substantially. So I got in and sat shotgun and JW drove because he had the directions.

Within ten minutes and two missed turns, we were in the HOOD. Utterly lost with no idea of how to get where we were going. Somehow all of that rehearsing and quizzing before we left was to no avail. So JW pulled into a 7/11 to get directions from God-only-knows-who was behind the counter, and I'm in the front seat trying to chat up an increasingly nervous Rock Star. He calmly said, "We're lost aren't we?"

I said, "NO!! No, no, no, no, no, we're not lost. We're taking a short cut, but we want to be sure that it's the right one!!" I don't think he believed me....

We eventually got back on the right road, sweat on our brows, and managed to get him to the airport on time. (I'm still not sure how we did it.) When we popped the question about working for him (not realizing that every college coach in the nation wanted the jobs we were asking for), he smiled, and laughed a little, and said, "Boys —I don't have anything for you, but I'll tell you what you do...." And he proceeded to give us advice, and walk us through the process of how to break in to the business. At the end of our conversation, he shook our hands very warmly, smiled, and said, "You guys remind me of myself when I was young. Keep at it. You'll do fine."

I never saw him again after that meeting, although I did talk to him on the phone once about a year later. When he picked up the phone I said, "Coach, this is Tim Shea!"

He said, "Yeah?"

Then I followed up with, "I took you to the airport in San Antonio after you gave the keynote address at the clinic."

Then he lit up, "OH HEY! HOW ARE YOU DOING TIM?! HOW'S IT GOING?!"

Here's a tip of the hat and a sincere thank you to Coach Kenny and to anybody who has ever stood on the top of the hill and, in looking down at the kids struggling to climb it, reached down to lend them a hand. Kenny didn't have to do that. It didn't help him in any way at all. But it made all the difference in the world to a couple of young, hungry college kids looking for a break. Thank you, Coach Ken Hatfield. You may never know how much that gesture meant to us. Then again...maybe you do.

▲ ▶ ▼ ▲ ▶ ▼ ▲ ▶ ▼ ▲ ▶ ▼ ▲ ▶ *Halloween Night*

Halloween night always brings back a flood of memories for me, some of them from my childhood and some of them from my parenthood, and all of them good. One such memory is from Halloween night in 2000. I had the pleasure of taking my then three-year-old out into the neighborhood for his first shot at trick-or-treating.

He decided early on that he wanted to be Batman, so his mom found him a Batman costume and a matching Robin costume for his little brother who was a little over a year old at the time. His mom found a great Cat Woman costume to round out the set, so, naturally, I was relegated to the role of Alfred Pennyworth, the butler. I was not about to rent a tux, so I left my suit on from work and called it good.

Robin had come down with a cold so it was his job to help his mama pass out candy. He didn't seem to care either way, and I'm not really sure that he fully appreciated the awesome responsibility that came with being Robin. But his brother didn't just dress up as Batman that night. He "became" Batman.

I can still see him in that little Batman costume. The top of his head came up to my thigh and he had to extend his arms all the way out just to carry his bag. He insisted on carrying his own bag though, because it was his, and he was going to do it himself. I can literally remember the conversation we had as we headed out the door and said goodbye to Cat Woman and Robin. I explained that we would go to each house on the block and ring the doorbell.

"Now buddy—do you know what to say when they answer the door?"

"HALLOWEEN!!"

"Nope. When they answer the door, you say, 'Trick or Treat.'"

"Oh."

"Try it."

"Trick a tree."

"Close. Trick or Treat."

"Trick or treat...?"

"Yep. That's it."

"OK."

It was a beautiful, crisp, moonlit, New Mexico night. There were a few clouds scattered in the sky, and they were illuminated by the moon. Most of the leaves were still on the trees in the neighborhood, and the aspen had all changed to that bright yellow-gold color that they get in the fall. I can still see it. I can even smell the air.

We both had a spring in our step from the weather and from the excitement of what was coming. When we got to the first door I lifted him up so that he could ring the bell (he had to do it), and he stood there patiently waiting, facing the door, with his bag at the ready. The nicest older woman answered the door, and he said his lines perfectly.

"Trick or Treat!"

"Well my goodness, it's Batman!"

"Uh-huh! And see my cape!"

"Oh my yes! Well let me get something for you."

And right then it occurred to me that I had forgotten to tell him about an important part of the ritual. When the woman walked back in to grab the candy, Batman followed her right into the house.

"Buddy, wait!"

It was too late. When she turned around to bring him the candy, he was standing right in the middle of her living room. I started apologizing all over the place and explaining that this was his first time out (of course I threw him under the bus), but she was laughing too hard to hear it anyway.

So he made his first score and turned to leave. I made sure that he thanked her before we left, and then we headed out to the next house.

"You did really good back there."

"This is fun!"

"Yeah, it is fun! Halloween is always fun. One tiny little small thing; from now on, we'll wait outside on the porch for the candy instead of going into the house, K?"

"OK."

So we worked the neighborhood like pros. We made good time, and we hit every house with a light on. I explained that the houses that were dark usually meant that either the people weren't home, or they didn't want to play Halloween.

"Why they don't wanna play?"

"I'm not sure, buddy. Maybe they're just tired and want to sleep."

"Maybe they already went Trick or Treat and they're eating their candy?"

"Yeah, maybe. But it's more fun to go at night."

"Yeah, I like going at night. Can we go tomorrow too?"

"No, pal. That's what makes Halloween so much fun. You only Trick or Treat on Halloween."

"When is another Halloween?"

"Next year. Same time."

"Oh."

"But we're gonna have fun tonight, right?"

"Yeah. This is fun. I like Halloween. I like being Batman, too."

"I like when you're Batman. It makes me feel safe."

"Yeah. I can guard us from bad guys. Is my cape still on?"

"Yep. Cape looks good."

"If I run will it fly in the wind?"

"Probably, but let's not run. We don't want to spill your candy. HOLY HALLOWEEN BATMAN!! We still have to get those houses over there!"

"HAHAHAHAHAHAHA Daddy, that was silly. Batman didn't say that...say it again."

"HOLY HALLOWEEN BATMAN!!!"

"HAHAHAHAHAHA!!! Are you havin' fun too, Daddy?"

"More than you'll ever know, buddy.... Or at least until you take your own kids out someday."

"Can I still be Batman then?"

"Sure—of course you can."

"Oh good. I always gonna be Batman."

"Yeah buddy, after tonight I think you'll always be Batman to me too."

▶▼▲ ▶▼▲ ▶▼▲ ▶▼▲ ▶▼▲ ▶ Guilt Trip Fail

I taught my guys the fine art of "ball-breaking" when they were very young. I was a hard kidder with them, but I always made sure that they knew I was kidding. So they learned the art form well. Too well. The following conversation occurred yesterday, in my car, when I picked up TJ from his mom's house:

"Hey Buddy! How are ya?! It's good to see you!"

"Good to see you too, Dadda!"

"I haven't seen you in a while."

"I know! I've been busy these last few weeks."

"I guess so. We should try to get all the time together that we can. I won't be around forever, ya know."

(Silence....)

"I mean, I'm gettin' older. I'll be dead before long, and then you're gonna feel horrible!"

"Dad...."

"Yeah?"

"The Italian guilt thing doesn't work for you."

"WHY NOT?!"

"'Cuz you're not Italian!!"

"WHAT'S THAT GOT TO DO WITH IT?!"

"Dad...I'm both Irish and Italian. I've seen both families."

"And?"

"Look—when we were picking out the music for Great-Nana's funeral, the whole family was crying just thinking about it!"

"Yeah...?"

"When you asked your dad what he wanted for his funeral, he said, 'I don't care—take me up to the reservoir and drop me in.' And then everybody laughed, including him!"

"Well...there is that."

"I'm hungry. Where are we goin' to eat?"

"You're always hungry."

"Dad, I'm a growing teenage boy. Besides, you're not gonna have me forever ya know...."

"Oh, knock it off."

▶▼▲▶▼▲▶▼▲▶▼▲▶▼▲▶▼▲▶▼▲▶▼▲▶ *Trevor*

When I was in college, I majored in education and at the end of my senior year I was assigned to a high school and to an elementary school to complete my K-12 student teaching. I was instructed to observe, make notes, ask questions, and generally get an idea of how things were done until I took my turn at teaching a section. In the elementary school, I was assigned to the fourth grade.

One morning, my supervising teacher pulled me aside and said, "You see that kid over in the corner? His name is Trevor. I can't do a thing with him. He's about two years behind in math and he's always been a problem. Take him aside and just see if you can do anything at all with him."

"Sure—what are you working on?"

"Times tables, through nine. If you can get him through three, it will be a huge improvement."

"OK, I'll see what I can do."

Trevor was a little African-American kid who didn't appear to have a lot of friends and even less self-esteem.

He rarely looked up, and when he did it was usually to meet a disapproving glare from a teacher or to catch a tongue-lashing about God-knows-what. When I walked over to him, he looked up at me and I saw fear and distrust in his eyes; a look that told me that he was anticipating yet another tongue-lashing, and that, again, he wouldn't know what for. So, I smiled at him and said, "Hey Trevor —my name is Mr. Shea... nah, bag that. My name is Tim, and today is your lucky day."

"It is?"

"Yep. I'm gonna let you in on a little secret. I'm the best teacher in the state of Texas," (I wasn't even close) "and I'm about to make you the smartest kid in this class-room."

The fear in his eyes slowly turned to curiosity, and he was willing to play along. "How you gonna do that?"

"I'm gonna show you that you know more than you think you do."

"Oh yeah?"

"Yeah. Take out your flash cards."

A little grin made its way across his face as he reached down into his backpack to pull them out. We started with a giant pile of the ones he didn't know, actually most of them, but as we went along we started making a small pile of the ones he did know. Very small. At first he was really discouraged, but as the "know" pile started to grow, his confidence grew with it, and so did his little smile.

"OK—let's do it again."

"AGAIN??"

"Yep. Do it."

So, after he let out a deep, I-can't-believe-we're-doing-this-again sigh, we did it again. And the 'know' pile kept growing. Then we did it again, and again, and again. When the class period was over, I said, "Trev—look at what you did. Do you see what I see?" Trevor saw it. He couldn't stop smiling as he nodded, and neither could I. The 'know' pile was the big one, and the 'don't know' pile only had a few cards in it.

"Take these cards home tonight, and do what we just did. Do it five times. Got it?"

"Yeah. OK, I will."

Three days later, I had mostly forgotten about it and I walked into the classroom to do my thing, when my normally reserved teacher met me at the door and said, "Come here!"

My first thought was, "Oh lord, what did I do now...?"

"What in THE hell did you do with that kid?!"

"What kid?"

"Trevor! That kid hasn't passed a math test all year and he just scored a 94 on his six weeks multiplication exam!"

"You're kidding...."

"What did you do?!"

"I sat down with him for 40 minutes and we just drilled flash cards. That's it."

"I can't believe it. I absolutely can't believe it."

I made a beeline for Trevor and said, "What's up with your test?"

Trevor didn't meet my eyes with fear that day. He met my eyes with pride and the biggest smile I had ever seen from him.

"I did good, huh?"

"Yeah, Trev. You did good. I told you that you knew this stuff. Now keep it going. I told you, you're the smartest kid in the class. You just didn't know it."

I didn't do a thing that day that anybody else couldn't have done. What struck me then, and has stayed with me all these years later, is that he was just as capable as any kid in that class but nobody had taken the time to show him. It wasn't about what he could do; it was about what he thought he could do.

I've wondered about him a lot over the years. I hope he has done well for himself. For all I know he could be in jail. For all I know, he could be working at NASA. What I do know is that I saw a ton of unlocked potential in that kid. And on that day, I think he saw it too. He did what he did on that math test and nobody could ever take that away from him.

▷▼▲▷▼▲▷▼▲▷▼▲▷ *Valentine's Dance*

One Friday or Saturday night, around Valentine's Day, the local community center put on a Valentine's Day dance for the kids. My guys, who were only in the 4th or 5th grade at the time, were in attendance and had a great time. I picked them up from the dance that night and got the full rundown on the way home. The director of the community center did a great job with it. The place was decorated, they had all the right music, and he made sure to set up several dances where kids were paired up and nobody was left out.

But there were a few free dances mixed in as well, where the kids could dance with whomever they wanted. My oldest son told me that after a few dances he spotted a girl who had been sitting by herself for a while and apparently hadn't been asked to dance. So he said, "I didn't really want to dance with her, but I walked over and asked her to dance anyway."

The way he described the situation to me, she was evidently not one of the popular kids. She was the kid who gets overlooked at dances. You know the kid I'm talking about. Some of you may have *been* that kid. *I* was that kid! So when I heard the story, I made a huge, big deal out of it. I really wanted to make an impression on him.

"T—I am SO PROUD OF YOU!! You have no idea of what that might have meant to that girl! I'm serious, buddy—things like that can leave an impression on a kid that they will never, in their whole life, forget! That is terrific! Good job!"

So, his younger brother, who was also at the dance, could see what was unfolding, and as he is intensely competitive, he was not going to be outdone.

"Dad, I did the same thing. There was this other girl who was by herself, and she was kinda shy and nobody was dancing with her, so I asked her to dance."

And again, I did the same thing. "Buddy, that's great!!! That's really great!!! I'm so glad that you weren't just thinking about yourself, but that you spotted a girl not having fun and you went up to her and asked her to dance!! Guys, I'm telling you...you just don't know how much of an effect that can have on a kid. She might remember that the whole rest of her life! You just never know! Great job! I'm proud of both of you!"

Then, I heard the line of the year from the mouth of my young one in the back seat.

"Dad...sometimes bein' a man means you have to dance with the ugly girls."

▶▼▲▶▼▲▶▼▲▶▼▲▶▼▲▶▼▲▶ *Coach O*

The man was a master motivator. He was the best I have ever seen at working the psychology of a football team. Of knowing exactly when to push, when to back off, and how far to do either one. He did it with individual players as well. He understood that different players responded to different types of coaching, and he knew our limits. Some responded to encouragement, some to teaching, and some to a good ass chewing. Personally, I always preferred encouragement. But my coach knew better. He always knew.

One day, during my senior year, I thought I was having a decent practice. I hadn't made any mistakes, I carried out my assignments and I wasn't getting beat. But on one particular play I heard an ear splitting, "SHEA!!! I AM GETTING SO SICK OF SEEING YOU...." and on it went. Right in front of the whole team. Up one side of me and down the other. He ripped me for a solid minute—which doesn't sound like much unless you're getting it. He finished with something like, "IF I DON'T SEE SOMETHING ON THIS PLAY, YOU ARE GONNA SIT FRIDAY NIGHT!!!!"

I was absolutely livid. I was furious. I didn't think I deserved it. What was this guy talking about?! After all I'd done, he just gave me one play to either earn my spot back or ride the pine on Friday night. On the upcoming play, I must confess that it was my full intention to hurt somebody. I mean, really, seriously hurt somebody. I dialed it in and I was going to make him sorry for it.

I had tears in my eyes when our scout team center snapped the ball. I ran over the top of the tackle across from me, then I ran over the top of the fullback who had stepped up to help him, and as I made a beeline for the quarterback, he literally dropped the ball and ran the other way. (I found out from a teammate about a year later that when Coach had finished chewing my ass before that play, he walked over to one of his assistants and whispered, "Watch this....")

The whole team was laughing, I still had tears in my eyes, and as I turned toward my coach to give him that, "How do ya like me now?!" look, he was grinning from ear to ear.

He walked up to me, and in a calm voice, said, "Shea," (he never called me Tim), "if you will play like that all the time, nobody can stop you." And then, as I tried to hide my tears from him, I realized that he had set me up. He had gotten so far into my head that he found the switch that I couldn't find, and flipped it himself. And he knew how to do that with all of us. Everybody who ever played for him has a similar story. A story of encouragement, of motivation, or of personal challenge.

He always had the pulse of his team. He knew when we were getting lazy, and he knew when we were getting fatigued. Two different things that can look a lot alike. Some days we would run 40-yard sprints after practice until we thought we were going to die. But once in a while, he would line us up at the goal line for sprints, and then he would say, "If you guys can be out of my sight in ten seconds, we won't run sprints." Talk about motivating a team to run sprints. We would run harder trying to get to the locker room in ten seconds than we ever would have run on that field—and laughed the whole way there. He always knew what we needed. He knew us as a team and as individuals. He knew us because he genuinely loved us.

During preseason practices, (two-a-days), he would beat us down to where we were dragging. But at the end of the two weeks of practices, every year, he would bring us together and talk to us about our progress and where we were as a team. And when he was done, he would finish by saying, "You know what's wrong with this team? Nothing. There is nothing wrong with this team. I would take this team, right here, over any other team in the state."

Then we would start to feel it. And he would keep going—telling us that he believed in us. Telling us how good we could be. He would come back with, "You know what's wrong with this team?"

The juniors and seniors—the guys who had heard it before—would shout back, "NOTHING!!!" And he would go on a little more.

Whenever he circled back to, "Do you know what's wrong with this team?!" we would all scream in unison, "NOTHING!!!!"

It became such a hallmark of his pregame motivational speech that we would wait for it. We knew it was coming, and we knew that it was the last thing he would say before he turned us loose onto the field. He would challenge us, motivate us, and sometimes even scare us. But just at the right time, he would get that wry grin on his face, break down and yell at the top of his lungs, "WHAT'S WRONG WITH THIS TEAM?!!!"

And we would scream back, "NOTHIN'!!!!"

Most of the time, all he could get out was "WHAT'S WRONG..." before we would jump in and scream, "NOTHING!!!" Then we would walk through the door, heads up and smiling as we made our way to the field.

I never played on a losing team in high school. In fact, I can count the number of games our teams lost, in three years, on one hand. We didn't have the best players. We had the best coach. A coach who knew how to get the very best out of us.

Coach was universally loved at Rocky Mountain High School. During the day, walking through the halls, he always had a smile on his face. He always talked to everybody he saw, and usually you could hear him laughing as he was talking. He had a unique manner of speaking, and every player on the team had a Coach O impression. We could all do him. Some better than others, but we all did him. We did him because we loved him. We really loved him.

One afternoon, in the spring of my senior year, he walked up to me as I was headed out to the shot ring for track practice. He said, "Tim, hold up a second." (He had never, in three years, called me Tim.) I'll never forget it. Ever. He said, "I just wanted to tell you that you've had a great three years here. You've done well in all your sports, you were a good student, and you were a pleasure to coach. I just wanted to tell you that."

I was stunned. I managed to eke out a "Thank you, Coach. It's been great and I've enjoyed playing for you." And then I turned away to try to hide my tears from him again.

Those simple words from a high school football coach will remain with me forever.

Yesterday I was informed that my beloved high school football coach, Patrick O'Donnell, died after a long battle with Alzheimer's disease. I was saddened to hear it, but at the same time relieved to know that he's free. I'm happy to know that it is finally his turn to walk through that door as one last time I try to hide my tears.

It makes me happy to imagine that as he walked through that door, head up and smiling, that he might have heard a voice from the other side saying, "You know what was wrong with the way you lived your life, Pat? Nothing."

I'll Be Here

▶▼▲▶▼▲▶▼▲▶▼▲

▼ ▲ ▶ ▼ ▲ ▶ ▼ ▲ ▶ ▼ ▲ ▶ ▼ ▲ ▶ ▼ ▲ ▶ *First Day*

Today was my youngest son's first day of high school. I've seen a lot of firsts come and go over the years, but the first day of school, for some reason, always hits me funny. I'm not sure how else to describe it. It leaves me, somehow, a little empty. His first day of school, in any year, always brings back memories of my own first day. And it happened again today. Right on cue. Today being his first day of high school took me back to his first day of kindergarten, which, in turn, took me back to my own.

It was an impactful day. I still remember it clearly. It impacted me like no other first day ever did because it was the day, the only day I ever remember, when my dad held my hand. He walked me all the way to school and told me about how much fun it was going to be. He told me about all of the new friends that I would make, and all of the things that I would learn there. I remember being apprehensive, but not afraid. I was nervous, because I didn't know what to expect.

When we got to school, he gave me a big smile and said, "Go get 'em buddy. I'll be here when you get out." I wanted to be brave for him, and for me, so I fought back a tear and just nodded. It was time to go, but what I really wanted was for things to stay the same. I wasn't ready to move on, but I had to. The time had come. So I fought back another tear, and held onto his hand until he let go of mine.

A generation later, I remember my son's first day of kindergarten. I remember walking him to school with his mom and me holding his hands as we went. We told him how much fun it would be and about all of the new friends he was going to make, and of all of the things that he would learn there. I remember being apprehensive, but not afraid. I was a little nervous because I didn't know what to expect.

When we got to school I remember smiling at him and wanting to be brave. I fought back a tear when I looked at him and told him how proud I was, and said, "Go get 'em buddy." And when it was time to go, what I really wanted was for things to stay the same. I wasn't really ready to move on, but I had to. The time had come. So when he turned to go, I fought back another tear, and held his hand, until he let go of mine.

This same memory comes back to me every year. Always on the first day of school.

At six years old, he and his little friends opened the back cage door of a dog catcher's truck to try to spring a special friend who had been captured—a Great Dane who roamed the town's streets at large, not really belonging to anyone, but belonging to everyone. The whole town knew that dog and they all loved him. The group of kids only wanted to free that one dog, but when they opened the door, every dog in the truck made a break for it at the same time—right over the top of the kids. He said that it looked like something out of an old cartoon. He was trampled; dogs took off in every direction with a group of six year olds right behind them, followed by an irate dog catcher.

At seven years old he got his first job pulling weeds in a bean field. He cried the whole first day, because he was convinced he would never see his home again. He and his friends got up before sunrise every morning and waited for a truck to stop by the corner and pick them up. He said that he knew the job had ended the day the truck didn't come by. That is how they were informed.

At ten years old he held down a job setting pins in a bowling alley. He would walk home after work at 11:00 p.m., and then start on his homework. Most nights he didn't get to bed before 2:00 a.m. He made average to poor grades in school. He never kept a dime of the money that he made as long as he lived at home. Whenever he received his paycheck, he turned it over to his mother without a second thought.

He spent the second half of his freshman year in high school in bed with an illness that went undiagnosed. He was so weak he couldn't get out of bed, but he managed to do enough school work to pass the grade. Years later, as an adult, he gave his medical history to a physician who guaranteed that he had had polio that year. He said, "I don't know why nobody ever thought of that. My friend, who lived next door, had polio." He came through it unscathed, but his friend was left in a brace and with a permanent limp.

When he went to college, he became enamored with the study of geology. His geology professor at the first school he attended helped him to transfer to the top rated school of geology in the country. He graduated with a near 4.0 GPA and #2 in his class. He also carried a double minor in physics and chemistry. He was offered a full ride scholarship to Cornell to pursue a Ph.D. but turned it down to go to work.

I asked him one time if he had any idea of why he had so many knee and back problems and he said that he thought that it started the night that he was on the deck of an oil rig in North Dakota, and had to jump off of it— two stories—for his life. A gas line had broken and was ignited by the heat from the drilling motor. He and one other man got off the deck just ahead of the fireball that took the lives of six men.

He started his consulting business with a personal loan from a wealthy friend and paid back every dime he borrowed, in the first year.

Despite making a good living in the oil business, and despite the urging and prodding of his friends, he always lived well below his means. He was a child of the Depression and, other than his house and his first car, he never bought anything for which he couldn't pay cash. He only owned one house in his life—the house in which I grew up, and he paid all of $22,000 for it. Fifty years later, my mother still lives in that house, and still misses the man with whom she made a life. I do too.

Today my dad would have been 86 years old. Here's remembering the ol' man and a life well lived. Slainte, Pop...

▶▼▲▶▼▲▶▼▲▶▼▲▶▼▲▶▼▲▶ *Full Tank*

I woke up this morning with a full tank. Completely full. The needle was just to the right of the big "F" on the gauge.

I have always enjoyed talking to my boys. We've been talking to one another since before they could use words. We've talked about all kinds of things over the years, from "What's that? What's that? What's that?" to "Why did they knock those buildings down?" to "My friend's dad just left them. He's never coming back. But after you go help Papa, you're coming back, right Dadda?"

Over the years, most of the talks made me laugh, a few of them made me think, and one or two concerned me for the moment. But they all made me thankful. Thankful to get to participate. Thankful that we could have the conversations at all. Thankful that they're thinking about things and interested enough to ask questions.

Last night I got to be in another one. My oldest sat down in front of me and said, "Dadda, I need to talk to you." That, right there, is what I call a "drop everything" moment. That is a hang up the phone, put down your pen, turn off the calculator, close the book and shut down the computer, moment. So I said, "Sure buddy—what's up?"

We sat together and had an amazing conversation. For over an hour, I listened to this kid tell me what was going on in his life, what he was thinking, why some of it was bothering him, and what he should do about it. I saw myself at 15. He's a lot like I was then, and he's also different. I threw in a couple of tidbits from experience here and there, but mostly I just let him talk.

I loved everything about it, but while we were talking I also got little, bittersweet snapshots of conversations gone by. I miss those. I miss asking him to tell me, just one more time, which Teletubbie is which and what do they do? I miss him thinking that I know everything. I'm starting to settle into "not getting it because it's all different now." It's fine. I don't mind it. My father didn't get it either. Neither did his father, or his father before him.

But last night, he seemed to think that I got it. As he told me about some of his friends and what they're going through, I mentioned some of my friends, who, at the same age, went through the same thing. I understood his perspective completely. I was in the exact same boat when I was 15, and the boats haven't changed. The seas really don't either. It's all the same stuff by a different name. And so we hammered it out; little man to big man; knee to knee, face to face.

When the conversation was finished, my little hulk of a son stood up and raised his arms above his head and said, "Get up Dadda, I gotta fill my tank."

Since they were babies I would tell my boys that I had to fill my tank, which meant that I needed one of those big, giant hugs that squeezes the breath out of me and lasts for days. So I stood up, pushed my chair back, and we filled our tanks. All the way full. I kissed him and told him how proud I am of him. He said, "Thanks Dadda. I'm gonna go to bed."

Last night I went to bed with a full tank. And this morning I woke up with a full tank. Completely full. All the way to the top.

▷▼▲ ▷▼▲ ▷▼▲ ▷▼▲ ▷ *My Father's Day*

As I sat at my desk and drank my coffee on this Father's Day morning, I had a chance to reflect on a few of the thousands of mental snapshots of my boys that I have stored away over the years—memories that go back to the moments of their births. TJ came out gray and floppy and almost didn't make it, and Nick came out pink and screaming. And on the days they were born, I held them and kissed them and told them how much I loved them.

I was there for their first steps, both from their mom to me, with that wide-eyed grin that seemed to say, "Are you seeing this?!"

I remember the silly make-up games I played with them while changing a diaper or getting them dressed. I remember being the lava monster in the living room that could only go on the rug but not up on the couch or the chair. (That was the rule.) Of course they would taunt me by jumping from one to the other. I remember the night we came up with the flying game, where they would jump off the stairs and into my arms at the bottom. They worked their way all the way to the landing at the top. Their mom wasn't present when we invented that game....

I vividly remember holding Nicky on my lap as he cried out a bad day when he was four years old. I remember singing 117 verses of Old McDonald with TJ on my lap in my big easy chair when he wouldn't go to sleep. After I went through the regular barnyard, I was adding tigers and elephants and dinosaurs and fish and every other thing I could think of just to keep the song going. It finally worked.

I remember coaching baseball games and football games and fidgeting in the stands during basketball games. I remember concerts where it was all I could do to keep the tears in my eyes from running down my cheeks. Sometimes I couldn't. I remember Christmas mornings, days at the pool, running after baseballs as they learned to play catch, school pictures, homework assignments, flashcards, playing DJ in the car with my CD collection as requests came from the back seat, and occasionally laughing so hard at something that one of them said that I almost had to pull the car over.

I remember a couple of times that I had to get heavy with one or both of them, and times in which a bad dream had one of them crowding me out of my own bed, and that all too familiar "parent panic" when one of them would go missing for a bit. I remember working with them as they learned to swim, teaching them to ride their bikes, and working pass patterns in the park.

As they've gotten older, I've had the pleasure of walking them through some of the bumps. First girlfriends that faded, how to handle a bully, how to look somebody in the eye when you speak to them and to offer them a firm grip when you shake their hand. We've talked about what to do when you're with a group of kids and things start to go bad. How to help a friend who just lost a parent. What to say to a friend who is starting down a bad path.

I've seen the look in their eyes when I know they're not buying it and I tell them, "Nothing is new under the sun, boys. It's all been done before. You didn't invent it—you just changed the names."

My two little hulks, one of whom is built like me and is as strong as a bull, and the other who has grown to about an inch taller than me, both still talk to me. They still like bouncing things off of me and hearing what I have to say about them.

Being a dad has been the single greatest blessing of my life. Bar none. I have enjoyed every minute of it. And for me, even all these years later, the real cherry on the sundae is still getting to occasionally hold them, kiss them and tell them how much I love them. Happy Father's Day to me. Happy indeed.

▶▼▲▶▼▲▶▼▲▶▼▲▶ *St. Patrick's Day*

St. Patrick's Day was my dad's favorite day of the year. He liked it better than any other holiday, as it allowed him to reach back to his Irish ancestry and celebrate his heritage and his family. He was as American as Uncle Sam, but was of Irish ancestry, and he was proud of it. He studied it and he knew a lot about it. So on March 17th, the birth date of the patron saint of Ireland, he would don his Irish cap and Irish sweater, and he would grab his Irish cane and head out to Mulligans for corned beef and cabbage, and a couple of drinks to make it complete. And, as this day this year was the first time St. Patrick's Day had come around since his passing, I decided to go into South Boston, (Southie), the historically Irish neighborhood in Boston, and commemorate the day in honor of my dad.

St. Patrick's Day in Southie is an all-day affair, and streets are closed all over the area. People show up by the tens of thousands sporting green beer, green wigs, T-Shirts, cups, glow sticks, hats, and whatever else they can find. But I came empty handed. I wasn't really sure of what

I was about that day, so I just kind of wandered around with a lost and empty feeling in my stomach until I came across this Irish pub called Shenanigans. I waited in line out on the sidewalk a while and chatted up my fellow revelers to kill the time. Everybody was in a good mood, most were feelin' no pain, and one young lady even picked up a string of beads she found lying on the sidewalk, staggered up to me, and put them around my neck. I wore them the rest of the day.

After I finally made it through the door, I ordered a shot of Jamison, listened to the Irish music that was playing overhead, made a few more friends, and generally had a very nice time. I toasted my Pop a few times, and as the afternoon gave way to late evening, I began to feel unsettled. Nothing was particularly wrong, but something wasn't right.

As I sat with it a while, I came to realize that I had never really taken the time to say goodbye to my dad. I mean when I got home, the day after he died, there were things to be done. We kids had to be strong for my mom, and there were arrangements to be made and some loose ends to tie up regarding my dad's business and financial affairs. My dad raised us, whether intentionally or not, to be emotionally tough. To be stoic. To do what needed to be done, regardless. All three of us, my sister included, are still that way.

So tonight I said goodbye to him; a year after the fact. I staggered a little as I said goodbye to my new friends, people I knew I would never see again, and made my way back to the train station. I still felt unsettled but I couldn't place it. I didn't feel sick, but it was coming from somewhere way, deep inside me. Then, without warning, a tear rolled down my left cheek and fell onto the sidewalk. Then another, and another. And then, almost as if somebody had flipped a switch, a year's worth of tears that I had held back, a year's worth of pain, came spilling out onto that sidewalk.

Most of the revelers had gone home by now and for the first time in a year I really, fully, realized that my dad had gone home too. I was alone on that sidewalk and I could feel it to my bones. But it was good. I needed to be alone at that moment. I don't know that I have ever cried that hard in my life. It had to happen. It was way overdue. It was painful and yet wonderfully cathartic. Floodgates that held back pain that had gone rancid were finally opened, and it all spilled out onto a lonely, open sidewalk in South Boston.

I think that from now on, this day will be a special day for me as it was for my dad. This day, St. Patrick's Day, will be the day that my dad and I get together to raise a glass to Ireland and to check in to say, "How are you gettin' along? I've missed you."

▼▲ ▶▼▲ ▶▼▲ ▶▼▲ ▶▼▲ ▶▼▲ ▶▼▲ ▶ *Stones*

God, in His mercy, granted me two sons. Two wonderful boys who are my whole life. Two wonderful boys who could not possibly be more different from each other.

TJ, the older of the two, has an outgoing, dynamic personality. He is full of confidence, has always been the most popular kid in his class, and is ambitious. He's had big dreams since he was very young, and I rather suspect that he'll reach his goals, whatever they may be. For now, he is in high school and most of his dreams center around his passion for football. He has played on his high school football team since he was a freshman, started a few games as a sophomore, and now starts both ways as a junior. He absolutely loves it. He is passionate about it, and I can honestly say, he's pretty good.

Nick, my youngest, is shy, quiet, and pensive. He prefers time alone and loves to analyze things and think deeply about them. He is amazingly creative, with an artistic bent toward music. He usually won't speak unless spoken to, but he is always polite, and, in his element, can be hilariously funny. He is the Yin to TJ's Yang. He has spent his life growing up in the shadow of a charismatic older brother. A long shadow at that. This is what brings me to the point of my story.

Early this summer, Nick came to me and said that he wanted to go out for football. He had played as a kid in a Pop Warner league, but then didn't play for a couple of years after that. He told me that as he got older and as the other kids got bigger, he got "scared." (I'm not sure why. He did very well when he played, and he's very athletic. But that's what happened.) But he decided that he wanted to try it again, and he came to me for some advice on what to do.

Football has been a great passion of mine since long before I was old enough to play on any organized team. I played in back yards, at the church across the street, in the park, or wherever a game was happening. The older kids in the neighborhood taught us how to play, and then pummeled us every chance they got. I went out for football the first year that I was eligible, and I played into my second year in college. After college, I went into coaching and did that for four years. I loved it. I still love it. So I was excited to hear that Nick wanted to give it another shot. I thought he had a real chance to be good, and I wanted him to experience some of the success and fun that his brother was having.

He went to work. He started working out with weights, and running. He did wind sprints on the football field and ran stadium stairs in the summer heat. He joined his team's preseason workouts and worked his butt off. Every time I would come to pick him up, he would be drenched in sweat, panting, flushed, and smiling. And he would tell me about what they did that day on the ride home. Everything was developing exactly as it should. He was working himself into shape, doing all the right things, and finally starting to taste the satisfaction that comes from totally spending oneself in the realization of a goal.

About three weeks ago, Nick came to me and said that he needed to talk. I dropped whatever I was doing, (something important, no doubt), and told him to have a seat. Then he dropped something on me that I didn't see coming. I could tell that he was nervous, and he stammered a little as he shared with me what he had been thinking. He told me that he had a change of heart. That he decided that football is not for him—that it's not his passion. He decided that even after all of the sweat and work that he put in, he just didn't want to play. In the face of an older brother who is obsessed with it, and a father who gave half of his life to it, he listened to that still, small voice inside that has always steered him along a different path, and he went with it.

I could not possibly have been more proud of him. I have always told my guys to find their passion, and pursue it with reckless abandon—I don't care what it is. And, I really don't. I stood up out of my chair, told him to stand up, and I hugged him. I told him that I was proud of him and that I wanted him to do whatever made him happy. So Nick will do exactly that. His passion, whatever it is, will take him along a very different path than mine. And you can bet that I will be on that path with him, cheering him on every step of the way, no matter where it leads.

▲ ▶▼▲ ▶▼▲ ▶▼▲ ▶ *Pennsylvania Avenue*

As I made my way east along I-90 through Northeast Ohio, I ventured off the interstate to Route 20 and made my way into my dad's hometown of Ashtabula. I had a little time and I wanted to revisit the house and town in which I spent several summers as a kid visiting my dad's family. I had no idea of what to expect when I got there, but I knew that years of memories from my childhood, and dozens of stories I heard from my dad's childhood, would come flooding back to me when I arrived.

As I made the turn off of Walnut and onto Pennsylvania Ave., I passed three or four houses and then saw it sitting there on the left side of the street, right where it should be. I parked out in front, on the other side of the street, and just sat there and looked at it a minute. I don't think I was more than nine or ten years old the last time I saw the place. It had been painted and was showing its age a little, but structurally it was exactly like I remembered it. The big, covered front porch where I would play with the few toys they had around, the gravel two-strip driveway, and the giant maple in the back yard.

I walked around the side of the house and looked up at the window to my dad's bedroom, the one he slept in when he was just a boy. The same one I slept in when we would visit during the summers when we would go back to see family. I continued around to the back, trying to be inconspicuous, and looked at the old screen door that led into the kitchen where my grandma would make sugar cookies for me. I can still see her standing in that kitchen and talking to me in that sweet voice of hers. The memories all came back. I guess they had never really gotten that far away.

I walked from there down the street to the hill that leads to the beach. I walked the same path that my brother and sister and I took when we were just kids, and the same path that my dad and his brother and sister took when they were just kids. The streets are still lined with the same trees that were standing there 40 years ago, the sidewalks, cracked and buckled, the air, moist and hazy, and the lake still stretching to the horizon. Just like I remembered it.

After spending some time on the beach, walking around and looking at the small stones smoothed out by eons of waves washing over them, and stepping over the occasional periwinkle shell, like the ones I collected as a kid, I walked back up to my car and drove down to the docks where ore ships used to come and go two at a time. My grandpa and my dad both worked on those docks. At one time they were the lifeblood of this little community, but they're all quiet now. Not a boat in sight. No loaders, no mountains of iron ore. It's all gone. Just a still, empty lot where a thriving industry once made its home.

I had sort of a melancholy feeling as I made my way out of town. Everyone in my family in that generation is gone now. My grandparents, my aunt and uncle, one of my cousins, my dad, and even the town itself, as I remember it. My dad's house is for sale now. The price has been reduced as there apparently are no buyers. You could spend more money for a decent automobile than they are asking for that house, but it needs work. My dad told me once that he couldn't imagine anybody having had a better childhood than he did. He had a million stories of that place, the house, the town, and the people in it, starting when he was no more than four or five years old, until the day he left home to join the Navy.

As I made my way back onto the interstate to continue my journey east, I put Ashtabula in my rearview mirror and I popped in a CD by Mark Knopfler, and I swear this is true; a song called "A Place Where We Used to Live" came on right at the following point in the song:

> *There used to be a little school here*
> *Where I learned to write my name,*
> *But time has been a little cruel here*
> *Time has no shame.*
> *It's just a place where we used to live*
> *It's just a place where we used to live.*

So, I did what any leather-tough, ex-jock would do in that situation; I swallowed hard, wiped my eyes, and headed down the interstate, leaving it, once again, behind me.

▼▲ ▶▼▲ ▶▼▲ ▶▼▲ ▶▼▲ ▶ *Mother's Day*

"Whatever else is unsure in this stinking dunghill of a world, a mother's love is not."

—James Joyce

For about seven or eight years I trained in the Japanese martial art of Shotokan Karate. I was fortunate to have studied under a Japanese instructor because he was able to teach us not only the stances and techniques, but also to translate some of the cultural origins behind them.

He drilled us over and over and over about the importance of stance. Of keeping the back leg planted firmly on the floor. Of grounding the entire body. The front leg could move. The front leg, or lead leg, would "venture out" from the base, but the base provided the power to the punches and kicks that we executed. Everything we did started from the base.

He compared it to a home. Keeping in mind that Shotokan came to Japan from Okinawa in 1922, and from China centuries before that, the culture was obviously different from that of 21st -century America. But the way that he explained it to us was that "The Father—the lead leg, ventures out from home to make a living. He must be mobile and light and quick. He must be able to adapt. This is his duty. The back leg is the base. That leg stays home and provides the foundation for the family. If the foundation is weak, the whole family is weak. That is her duty. To ground the family."

On this Mother's Day, I want to recognize and thank the base of our family for being the foundation and stabilizing force that propelled the family forward.

My mom was one of 13 children, born in the farmhouse in which she was raised, and raised, by today's standards, in abject poverty. The kids slept four to a bed, with her bedroom doubling as a storage room for grain sacks. She was born with an uncanny musical talent, which she developed, and which allowed her to enter and win music contests as a teenager. Her talent also allowed her to make a living as a professional piano player with an acting troupe in Denver.

She met my dad in Denver, got married, and was blessed with three colicky babies, one right after the other. (I'm given to believe that the birth of the oldest almost prevented the birth of his two siblings.)

It was then that this farm-raised, country tough, foundation of the family, dug in and created the power base from which the rest of us moved forward. It wasn't flashy, but the base leg never is. It is the support beam which allows the lead leg and the arms to "do the karate."

My dad traveled a lot on business when we were young. In the early days he had no choice. So my mom was left to hold it all together. I always knew that she missed him when he was gone. I could see it, even then. But she never complained. Not once. Sometimes when things were getting a little stale, she would ask us if we wanted to go to Rob's drive-in for dinner. That was a big deal. Money was short then and that was fun food—for no reason at all. We had food at the house, but she knew when Rob's was in order, wild extravagance or not.

She also knew when a game of Crazy Eights or Old Maid was in order. Once in a great while, when my dad was home, we would all play, and we never laughed harder than when my mom would have to keep going back to the deck to get a match. I think one time she drew 15 straight cards, and we almost wet ourselves laughing. And for our benefit, she really leaned into it. She played it up. I remember that so clearly that I could literally show you where each of us was sitting that night.

When we were young and things went bump in the night, we all knew which side of the bed mom slept on. That side was the gateway to safety. There wasn't a monster in the world that could get to us in that bed. The safest I've ever felt in my life was when I slept between mom and dad. Neither of them slept, of course, but I did. I slept like a baby.

I think that moms receive some kind of gift when their children are born. (Make no mistake; mothers who adopt children receive the same gift.) It's a gift of somehow, instinctively knowing when something isn't right. They sense it. They can read their kids' faces like billboards. Sometimes they don't even have to see them to know.

I can think of at least twice while growing up when I was dealing with something heavy, that my mom would see it in my face (I never talked about it), and then about a day later, my dad would bring it up, because *somehow* he suddenly saw it.

Several years ago, she called me one morning, out of the blue, to ask me what was wrong. I hadn't talked to her in at least a week, and I said, "Nothing. Everything's fine."

And she said, "No. Something happened. What was it?"

Sure enough—something had happened. Something pretty big. And she knew it before I had said a word. I guess it's a mom thing. And mine got it in spades.

My mom is not hard. Quite the contrary actually, but she is tough. The way she grew up, she had to be. They didn't cry about things on the farm, they just dealt with them and moved on.

I've only seen my mom actually cry three times in my life. Think about that a minute. Three times in 54 years.

Once when my dad's mother died. Once when our puppy was hit by a car and killed. And once when she thought she had lost me.

See, I grew up in a safe neighborhood at a safe time and kids went out and played for hours on end never bothering to check in at all. We just had to be home before the street lights came on. But one summer night when I was about six years old, I came home through the back door and went downstairs and flipped on the TV. For whatever reason I didn't bother to announce my presence, and my mom didn't know I had come home.

As the day gave way to evening and the streetlights had long since come on, she went out looking for me. She drove up one street and down the next. She looked in parks, backyards, and every place else she could think of, and when she got home she was crying. She yelled downstairs for me, and I yelled back, and then when I saw her, I started crying. (When my dad found out what had happened, he was none too pleased with me, and I announced my presence in the house from that day forward.)

I guess that all of this is really just to say that while the base, the foundation of the unit, mostly goes unnoticed...I noticed it. I've seen it for years, and I wanted to recognize my mother for being the power leg that propelled our family forward. My dad became a nationally-recognized geologist, my brother and sister and I won awards for various things, and my mom quietly, from the shadows, provided the launching pad, the power base, that allowed it all to happen.

I love you Mama. Happy Mother's Day.

(P.S. No worries. I may be out of sight sometimes, but you'll never lose me.)

▲ ▶ ▼ ▲ ▶ ▼ ▲ ▶ ▼ ▲ ▶ ▼ ▲ ▶ *Two Years Later*

Two years ago today, my pop departed this world for parts unknown. He loved his life and would have lived it again ten times over if he could have, but toward the end he was ready to wrap it up. For three or four years he couldn't sleep, he was in a lot of pain and there was no longer anything in the course of day to day life which held his interest.

He loved his wife to the last day, and he loved his kids and looked forward to seeing us, but with lives and families of our own, we couldn't get back to visit as much as we would have liked. He understood that and he was fine with it. To him, that was the natural way of things. We were to grow up, leave home, and start lives and families of our own.

He was always very matter of fact about things, death included. He didn't believe in sugar-coating anything. In his last year he said to me once, "I'm not a bit afraid to die. To be honest, I'm looking forward to it."

But, I don't really think a lot about the "sick days" when I think about him. Those days were brutally hard and he wasn't himself anyway. I think about my dad the way I knew him when I was growing up. The way I knew him when I was a teen and a young adult. He was engaged and bright-eyed and curious and always optimistic. And he had a million stories.

A few years ago my mother turned the bedroom that my brother and I shared as kids into a little TV room. It's just big enough for a couple of chairs, separated by a lamp stand, a little desk off to the side, and a TV cubby against the wall. It is the perfect room for sitting and watching TV or just sitting with the TV on and talking about nothing at all. Every time I would come back to visit, my dad and I would sit in that room together and do exactly that, sometimes for hours on end. Just sit with the TV on and talk about nothing. He would ask me how my car was running. He would ask me about the weather where I lived, how the boys were doing, how the job was going, what my friends were up to—just, really nothing.

But invariably, at some point in the middle of all of that nothing, something would come up that would take our conversation off of the smooth, big, monotonous highway that we were on and lead us off onto a little road that would take me to a place I had never been before. And it was on those little roads and in those places that he would drop the gold nuggets. Little nuggets that I wouldn't have gotten any other way. Little nuggets about his childhood, his time in the Navy, his time in college, his business, or once in a while, even something about his impressions of raising a young family.

He told me about how his tiny high school band won the state band contest in a division in which they weren't even allowed to compete because they were too small. So the band director recruited extra kids from the high school to fill in the number of players required to compete with the biggest and best, and then gave them instruments stuffed with rags. He told them to hold them up to their mouths and blow, but not to make any sound.

He told me about the night in Hong Kong when a bunch of his Navy buddies found him in a tattoo parlor, three sheets to the wind and ready to be inked, but they knew he never wanted that. So they went in after him and had to fight their way out of the place with him literally on their shoulders, kicking and protesting the whole way. He went around the ship and thanked every one of them the next day.

He told me about the night he almost died on an oil platform in North Dakota, about meeting Joe Lewis, the World Champion Boxer, and about the friends that he lost as a kid who drowned in Lake Erie not two blocks from his house. He told me about hitchhiking with bags full of money that he had collected from his paper route and about the stray terrier that he adopted and trained to drop papers on the porches for him. Everybody in town knew that dog and most were afraid of him, but my dad made him mind, and the dog loved him for it. The dog was fiercely loyal and that loyalty saved my dad from being chewed up by a Great Dane one afternoon. That little Airedale terrier waded into the Great Dane and sent him out of the fight on three legs and yelping.

He told me about the time that he took a summer job in a factory putting car brakes together by hand, and how one of the union workers tried to slow him down because he was making the other guys look bad. My dad was being paid by the piece and he was there to make money so he didn't slow down. When the guy tried to lean on him to slow it down, my dad dumped him into a drum full of brake grease and left him. He said that he thinks the guy's buddies pulled him out but he couldn't be sure. He never had any trouble after that.

I learned about why he didn't eat apples, about how his dad was offered a contract with the Cleveland Indians, about his uncle walking out of the house and down the street for a pack of cigarettes and then returning home two years later like nothing had happened. I heard his indelicate opinions about religion and politics and a few about family friends from days gone by that would make me double over with laughter. I heard a thousand stories in that little room, all just awaiting the opportunity to be told. Stories about nothing. Stories from a life well lived.

And then, as quickly as we veered off of it, we would get back onto the main road, as if we hadn't taken the detour at all.

"What's Oklahoma gonna have this year?"

"What do you hear about the Broncos?"

"I think I might make a pot of that chili today. You like that chili don't you?"

He got a lot softer in his old age than he was when we were young. A lot quicker with a smile and a laugh. He would flirt with the girls at the bank, the post office, Mulligans, the doctor's office, everywhere he went. And they all loved him. After my dad died, his physician sent a personal note to my mom saying what a pleasure it was to have known him all of those years. I was told that one of the girls at the bank cried when she heard the news. I like to think that most everybody who knew him was going to miss him, at least a little.

The last time I saw him, he was lying in a bed in a rehab center with his eyes closed. I had to leave to catch a plane, but I told him that I would call when I got home and that I'd be back out to see him again as soon as I could. Not being one for drama, he just raised his arm and said, "All right Timmer, I'll see you later."

And that was it. Those were the last words he ever spoke to me. Like I was just headed down the street to a hotel but would be back the next day for breakfast. I knew he was on his way out, and so did he. But he wasn't going to make a big deal out of it. That was just him.

I was blessed far beyond what I knew at the time to have had him as my dad. It's funny; as close as we were, I'm not a lot like him. I don't think like he did, and I place a higher value on different things than he did. But we were always close. In all of the years we were together, we never had a problem to speak of. Granted, he didn't really allow problems, so that was part of it, but I never wanted a problem with him. Never looked for one. I wanted his advice, his opinions, his reassurance, his companionship, and sometimes just the sound of his voice.

Two years later, nothing has changed. I still want all those same things.

▷▼▲▷▼▲▷▼▲▷▼▲▷▼▲▷ *Still Listening*

I remember walking into my living room after dinner one night when I was young, and finding my dad sitting in his big easy chair, listening to a song by some Irish tenor. It wasn't unusual, as he loved music, but he had kind of a faraway look on his face as he was listening. That was unusual. My dad wasn't given to emotion, but the song seemed to move him.

He looked my way when I came in and asked me what I had been up to. We chatted for a few seconds and then I asked him what he was listening to. He told me who the guy was and when I asked him about the song, he said, "Oh...it's just a song about an old man worrying about his son coming home, and then hearing his voice."

"His voice?"

"Like when you stay out past dark and then I hear you come in." And that was all he said about it.

Every parent of a kid old enough to be out unsupervised knows this feeling. You tell yourself that everything is fine, while at the same time you fight off the images of every conceivable thing that is not fine. You just want to know that they're all right. It comes with the territory.

But as my dad was not particularly given to dropping his guard, even a little, and exposing his feelings about things, it hadn't occurred to me that he really worried about me at all. I mean, I always knew I was all right. I figured that he did too. But maybe he did worry a little. Just like I worry about my guys now from time to time. Maybe he worried a little, but was just careful not to show it. Or maybe he just didn't know how.

Maybe my ol' man listened for the sound of my voice my whole life and I just never realized it. In the morning when I stumbled out of bed, and again at night when I came in from the day. Maybe he waited just to hear my voice over the phone after I had moved out and gone on to college. Maybe he just wanted to know that I was all right. Once in a while, after I was old enough to drive, I would stop by his office on the way home, just to pop in and say hi. I always hollered from the door before he could see me from his desk. He seemed to like that. I know that the sound of my boys' voices, and knowing they're all right, means everything to me. I love it when one of them calls me to tell me something, important or not. Maybe my dad was no different.

Now, as an adult looking back on what he said to me after listening to that maudlin Irish tenor singing about his son, it occurs to me that he was no different from me. From any of us. He probably did listen for the sound of my voice. He must have. Sometimes I wonder if he still listens.

Today, on the third anniversary of your passing, Pop, I just wanted to check in and let you know that I'm here and I'm all right. Things are fine. I still miss you, and I'll always love you.

100

I wanted to check in, especially today.

Just, on the off chance, that you might be somewhere, still listening for the sound of my voice.

▲ ▶ ▼ ▲ ▶ ▼ ▲ ▶ ▼ ▲ ▶ Tales from the Bridge

As T and I headed back east across the Tobin Bridge this morning our conversation meandered across different lines until it found its way to girls and dating and all that that entails. He was in his early teens and his limited experiences and interests were ripe for harvesting some great conversations. He was talking about some of the girls that he knew and as I asked about them, the conversation worked its way to qualities to look for in a woman and in a relationship. I assure you, I am no expert, but I told him what I thought was right and I explained that these qualities are, of course, predicated on being a good enough man to be worthy of them, and to never take either one for granted.

He seemed to get it but went on to say, "Dad, I'm not sure I can see having a girlfriend. They're expensive!"

"Oh yeah?"

"Yeah!! I mean, you're paying for everything, right?"

"Sure. You never let a woman pull out money on a date."

"Right. So, everything you buy is doubled, and YOU KNOW HOW MUCH MOVIES COST NOW?!"

"Oh yeah. It's expensive."

"Well yeah, now they are! But, I mean, what were movies when you were my age? A nickel?"

"A NICKLE?! Are you high?! That's what they were when your grandpa was a kid! I paid $3.00 a ticket when I was your age!"

"$3.00?! You take a girl to a movie and get her pop-corn and a coke and you're out $50.00 now!"

"Tell me about it.... But, you gotta remember, I was only makin' $3.00 an hour in those days."

"Are you serious?"

"Oh sure. And I wasn't working at a swimming pool either! You know what I was doing at your age?!"

"Oh, here we go...."

"I was swingin' a pickaxe and literally diggin' ditches with a sharpshooter and a spade!"

"Where are my headphones?"

"You ever operate a jack-hammer at 6:00am?!"

"Ah...here they are."

"I was layin' copper pipe in commercial buildings and backfilling holes with a shovel because my boss was too cheap to spring for a backhoe!"

"Dad...WHY WOULD YOU TAKE A JOB LIKE THAT?!"

"You took what was available then, and I didn't have a swimming pool and pizza shack to work at!"

"Oh, here's a good song...."

"You kids have it too easy. That's the whole problem right there!"

"We're almost home, right?"

"You have any idea of how much a wheelbarrow of wet cement weighs? And on top of that, how hard it is to wheel that thing across a construction site on uneven, hard-packed dirt?! I had callouses on my callouses! I'm telling you...."

(Now, he's singing along with the song on his head-phones to drown me out. So I did what any other Father-of-the-Year recipient would do; I reached over and snapped his headphone against his ear.)

"OW!!!! Dad, did you ever have to hear this same lec-ture from your dad, about how soft you were and how much harder he had it than you?"

And in thinking about it a moment—it stopped me in my tracks. Then it made me smile.

"Yeah, buddy. Come to think of it, I did. I surely did."

▼▲ ▶▼▲ ▶▼▲ ▶▼▲ ▶ *The Birthday Volley*

My dad endured a birthday wish like a root canal. He knew that it had to be done and he was always a good sport about it, but he didn't look forward to it. He would accept it, thank the greeter, and then immediately turn the conversation back to whoever had called or stopped by. It didn't matter who it was. The same held true with his family. It was a formality to get through as quickly as possible, and then on to other things.

So every year, my dad and I would go through the same ritual. Every year, on this day, I would get through my work day, and then I would call to wish him a happy birthday. After I said my lines, he would say his, and then he would turn the conversation back to me. He would ask about my job, the boys, the weather—whatever. Just something to get the focus off of him and onto me. Every year.

For the better part of the day today, the thought of calling my dad and wishing him a happy birthday came and went. I was missing the ritual—the back and forth—

and really, I guess, just missing him. Toward the end of the day, as I was wrapping up work, the thought of calling him popped back into the front of my brain and wouldn't leave. This was about the time that I would have called him, and he would have been waiting for it. So, I just sat with it a bit. Wanting to connect again, but knowing that I couldn't. I thought a little about what I might tell him about what was new after he had volleyed the ball back into my court. And I even thought about what he might say in return. I just sort of played out the conversation in my mind.

About that time, in fact, at almost exactly that time, I received a text message from my son that said, "Call me when you can." I don't get many of those from him so I called him right away.

"Hey buddy—just got your note. What's up? Everything all right?"

"Yeah! Dad, I'm gonna get right to it...I just found out that I was voted All-Conference as Defensive Tackle!!"

"You just found this out? Today?"

"Yeah, at the school assembly!"

Really.... Today— of all days. I received this text at the end of the work day, just as I was wrapping up and getting ready to make the call that I knew I couldn't make, and could never make again.

Looks like the 'ol man found a way to do it again. Just as I was wishing him a happy birthday, he flipped it back on me. This time, he didn't even have to ask what was new. He found out before I did. But I think he would like to have heard me tell him the news anyway.

"Hey Pop—guess what I found out today...!"

Happy Birthday, Dad. I still miss you, and I'll never forget.

▷▼▲▷▼▲▷▼▲▷▼▲▷ *Christmas Letter*

It was a quiet Christmas morning here today. Mom and I had some breakfast together and spent a little time afterward chatting over coffee, about this and that. Nothing in particular. She asked me if I still like the new phone that she got me yesterday, and I told her again that I still love it. I was in dire need of a new cell phone and Mom came through in the clutch, like she always does.

After we finished up breakfast, Mom went back to her newspaper and I retired to the little TV room that doubled as my dad's home office, and sat down in the old rocking chair next to the desk. I grabbed a huge file of papers that Mom had pulled out for me the night before, and decided that now was as good a time as any to go through it.

It was filled to overflowing with old letters, pictures and various odds and ends that my parents had saved over the years. I pulled out copies of emails that they had printed out and saved, little pictures that the boys had drawn when they were in preschool, and a few old photographs. Some of them I vaguely remembered, and others

I remembered as if I had sent them yesterday. I was probably in there for an hour or two, just taking my time and reliving each moment as it came from that file.

When I had gone through everything in the file and just as I was about to close it up, I noticed, at the very back, down at the bottom, an envelope, addressed in my handwriting, to my dad. It contained a letter that I had written to him in 1989. I knew immediately what it was and my heart leapt into my throat as I took it out to read it. It was a deeply personal letter in which I poured out a page and a half of the kinds of things that we never talked about in my family. The kinds of things that we never said to each other, even though we all felt them. That's just how we were.

I still remember the day that I wrote that letter to him. I had just heard a song on the radio by a group called Mike and the Mechanics, entitled, "In the Living Years," and I decided then that I had to get my thoughts and feelings on paper and send it off before reason took over and I changed my mind. So I did. I knew while I was writing it, that my dad would be uncomfortable with the letter, but I needed to tell him things that I couldn't have told him to his face. Like how he had always been my hero, and how much I loved him, and how proud I was to be his son. I told him about how one day I would brag about him to the kids that I might have and how I had always tried to follow his example.

In person, he wouldn't have known how to react, or even what to do with it. He would have been embarrassed and what I was trying to tell him would have been lost. He just wasn't wired for it. So I poured it all out in that letter and I didn't hold anything back.

He never let me know what he thought about the letter or if he had even received it. So when I saw him about six months later I mentioned it to him in a casual conversation and he just said, "Yeah...I've got it."

And no other words were ever spoken about it. He had a way of letting you know that a conversation was over before it started, and this was clearly one of those conversations. So I let it go. I had to be satisfied that I had told him what I needed to tell him but could never have told him to his face. And the subject never came up again.

I suppose I've thought about that letter a few dozen times over the years, and each time wondering if he really "got" it. Wondering if it communicated what I had hoped it would. With my dad it was hard to tell. But I never once regretted writing it, and I'd do it again under the same circumstances. I would let him know how I felt about him and hope, as I did then, that the message got through his tough exterior and touched something down deep. Maybe that unique thing that a father has for his son. I never knew—until today.

This Christmas morning, 25 years after I wrote that letter, I found it. I found it tucked safely away in a file containing the pictures and drawings and emails that were special enough to him to keep forever.

And today I got my answer. Today, Christmas morning, he gave it back to me.

▼ ▲ ▷ ▼ ▲ ▷ ▼ ▲ ▷ ▼ ▲ ▷ *It's Been a Goodin*

For the past week now, my extended family and I have been processing the passing of one of the funniest, most genuine men I have ever known in my life. My Uncle Don Douglas passed away on September 11, and things just haven't been right since. I suspect that they won't be for quite some time.

My Uncle Don once said that the invention of the smart phone was the end of the great sea stories, because with the invention of smart phones, it was too easy to check the facts. I think he had a point. And, being as I am a member of a large extended family on my mother's side, most of whom knew my uncle better than I did, I'll keep this remembrance to impressions and direct experience with him, lest I get called out by one (or all) of my many relatives for getting a story wrong.

My Uncle Don was born the fifth child and first boy to a family of 13 children. He was raised in what we would now call abject poverty, during the Depression, in a farm house with no electricity, no indoor plumbing, and where the kids slept four to a bed. They wore hand-me-down clothes, most of which had been mended many times over, and did without extravagances of any kind. They were dirt poor but managed a happy and loving home despite it.

Uncle Don told story after story of growing up in that time, and usually included details of how hard it was, but every story, every last one, involved either a great memory or a funny one. I don't think he ever knew a bad day. He was just that kind of guy. I heard stories about his brothers, his grandfather, working on the farm, riding stick horses to school (which they would tether about a quarter mile from the school so as not to scare the other kids), and following the tops of fence posts when it would snow, which he later swore were telephone poles.

He worked hard all his life, joined the Navy as a teenager and saw a lot of action in the South Pacific. After returning home, he met his future wife at a community dance. The story he told was that he spotted her across the room and told his buddy that he was going to turn up the charm and go talk to her. Sixty or seventy-something years later, he was retelling that story and said, "I must have had it turned up too high, 'cuz she's still with me."

In a really big family, you can't sit around the table and talk because there's not enough room. So the family, when the weather would allow, would adjourn to the back yard at Grandma's house and set up lawn chairs in a circle. And they would talk for hours. And then when another one of the brothers or sisters would show up, somebody would say, "Well, look who's here!" and the whole family would adjust the chairs out to widen the circle and create a space. And then a while later it would happen again. It became known to us as the "Douglas Circle."

This went on all afternoon and into the evening. Story after story after story. Everybody had at least one, and most everybody could pitch in to all of them. By the time everybody showed up, that circle would cover about a quarter of an acre, but it didn't matter. The stories kept going and Uncle Don would still be in his same chair, farther out from the center, but still holding court. Somehow, he always ended up as the center of attention. He always seemed to have the best stories. They kept coming, and we just kept laughing.

His stories, and moreover, the way he told them, landed him gigs as MC at several social events. As I remember, he even occasionally filled in for the preacher at the local Methodist church. I remember one Sunday he came into Grandma's house after doing so, and somebody asked him how it went. He filled his coffee cup and said, "Those poor sinners are still in the church cryin' and repentin'."

He and his family lived in a modest but nice house on a fairly large plot of land at the edge of town. To maintain it, he had a lawn tractor that he used for mowing, and my brother and I loved that thing. He knew it, too. He used to invent little projects for us, which somehow always included that lawn tractor. Move that trailer over there. Put these blocks on the back and drive them to the barn. Whatever. He would tell us that he needed us to come mow his lawn for him and then patiently explained to us how to do it. His lawn always looked like somebody had run buffalo through it when we were done, but he never said a word about it. He just told us that it would need mowing again next week.

When his daughters left for college, he began writing them a sort of newsletter on the computer. He called it his Daily Constitutional, and it was pretty much just the goings on in their little farming village of 375-400 people, give or take. And as I understand it, the girls would share it with their roommates, then their dorm mates and then they, in turn, would subscribe. He just added them to the distribution list and kept going.

Over the years he gained more and more subscribers until he literally had people all over the country—people he had never met—reading this thing every day. It was quite a lot like Garrison Keillor's "News from Lake Wobegon." As the stories from around town dried up, or it happened to be a slow week, he would take a trip down memory lane. And then came the stories of his childhood, and the war, and selling grain bins to farmers, and every other thing he could think of. The stories were priceless. People would open their email first thing in the morning just to get the Constitutional to start their days.

The stories were so good, in fact, that in his late eighties, a neighboring town's newspaper editor asked him to write a column for them. So he did. The same, exact stuff he had been doing all along. Just little stories about life in a small town and his trips down memory lane. The column became wildly popular.

A few weeks ago, he wrote all of us through his newsletter and told us that he had just been to the doctor and found out that he "has cancer in just about every organ there is." When the doctor asked him what he wanted to do about it, he said, "Nothing." He was 90 years old, and a few weeks later he left us.

The Douglas circle has tightened up over the years, as we've had to remove chairs, one at a time, and put them up for good. Most of the kids have left town and started lives and families of their own. Some of their kids have kids now. But the last chair we moved out and folded up seems to have been harder, somehow. It's not to say that we haven't missed everyone who left us. We certainly do. But somehow this one seems different. Uncle Don was the ringmaster. He was the spark plug of the group. The one you could hear coming down Grandma's gravel driveway before you saw him, and carrying two or three lawn chairs in each arm for whomever else might show up. I never saw him without a smile on his face or without a story just waiting to be told. God, how I am going to miss those stories.

At the top of the newsletter he sent us, informing us of his illness, he simply wrote the words, "It's been a Good-in." He had no complaints, no regrets, and faced the end with the same optimistic, grateful attitude, with which he faced every day of his life.

I like to think that my grandparents, aunts, uncles, and cousins who have gone on before are all sitting around a new circle now, and telling stories and laughing, just like they did at Grandma's house. And that seven days ago, somebody looked up and said, "Well look who's here!" And they all got up and widened the circle again.

Detour Ahead

▶▼▲▶▼▲▶▼▲▶▼▲▶▼▲

▶▼▲▶▼▲▶▼▲▶▼▲▶▼▲▶ *Ever Vigilant*

Ever meet that guy that takes his job just a little too seriously? I mean, sure, you want doctors and lawyers and pilots and...well, everybody, to take their jobs seriously. But I mean the guy that really goes over the top, for a job that could be done away with and nobody would know the difference. That guy. Well, if you don't know him, it's because today he was in Boston, Massachusetts, working for a security company. His job appeared to be securing either a parking lot, loading dock, or a building—the outside of it—and he was going to do it at all costs. And, in fact, he did.

I met that guy today, about ten hours into my work day and I hadn't had lunch yet. Or for that matter, breakfast. I wasn't at my best, I'll leave it at that. As I was unloading empty 55-gallon steel drums onto a sidewalk to transfer into a storage area, this kid walks up to me, in full security detail uniform, and says, "SOOOooooooo... why are you putting these drums here on my sidewalk?"

He was all of 20 years old and a buck thirty soakin' wet. He had on a hat, a badge, a uniform, and one of those radios that attach at the shoulder.

"Your sidewalk....??"

"That's right. What are you doing here?"

"I'm off-loading these drums to take them inside."

"Why are you doing that?"

(He just stepped on my last hungry, surly nerve.)

"Because the truck won't fit through the door."

"Stay right there sir, I need to check this out. Patrol 2 to base, come in base."

(..........Are you kiddin' me..........???)

And over his radio I hear something like, "Gozzzzhttttt twzzzzz."

"Uh yeaaaaaaaaaah, I gotta guy, says he's a truck driver, and needs to bring some large, unmarked barrels into the facility, over...."

"Bzzzzzzzzzzzztttttttttt, Ffffffffftttttttttttzzzzzzzzzz copy."

"Roger that, base. Stand by. Sir, I'm gonna need you to step over here."

"No."

"No?"

"No."

"Why not?"

"Because I'm working, and I can hear you fine from here."

"Yeeeeeeeeeeeaaaaaaaaaaaahhh. Uh, sir, just what are you going to do with these barrels?"

"You see that door right there? I'm going to take them through that door—one at a time. Then I'm going to take some full ones out of that same door, and put them on this big truck that you see... right here."

"OK, stay right there, please."

"No."

"Patrol 2 to base, come in base." (And he repeated what I told him with a sort of smarmy tone, possibly to suggest that I was up to no good.)

"Bzzzzzzttttttttt-RAAAFFLLLLMMMMMOOOOOM-MMMBEEERRRRRR POPPITTT!!!!!!"

"Copy that base."

"Sir I'm gonna need some information. Is this your vehicle?"

"You mean this giant thing here that I'm taking the drums off of?"

"Uh...yeah."

"Yes. This would be my vehicle."

"Sir, who do you work for?"

"See that name on the side of the truck? That's who I work for."

So now, he takes out a little notebook and says, "Sir could you spell the name of the company please?"

"No."

"Sir, why not?"

"BECAUSE IT'S SPELLED OUT ON THE DOOR NOT FIVE FEET FROM WHERE YOU'RE STANDING!!!!"

"Oh.... Patrol 2 to base, I have an affirmative I.D. on that truck. Sir, are you the driver of the truck?"

"Are you kiddin' me?"

"Oh...yeah. OK. How long are you going to be here?"

"It depends on how long you insist on talking to me."

"Right. OK. Let's keep things moving here. I need to keep this area clear."

"It's a loading area. This is what it's for."

"Well...yeah, but I gotta keep it clear."

"For what??"

"For trucks that ha...."

"What??"

"Never mind. I just had to check it out."

"Check what out?"

"Uh...right. OK, you're free to go."

"I'm not going anywhere."

"Oh. Well, then just go ahead and move the drums."

"Out of curiosity—are you new here?"

"Well, yeah...kinda."

"Fair enough. One more thing; you ever heard of Barney Fife?"

"Barney who?"

"Never mind. He was before your time."

▲ ▶ ▼ ▲ ▶ ▼ ▲ ▶ ▼ ▲ ▶ ▼ ▲ ▶ *Blossom Street*

I was wondering if I could get a prayer, or a positive thought, or a moment of silence, or good energy, or whatever it is you like to do, for an elderly gentleman and his daughter who are staying in a hotel across the street from one of the finest hospitals in the country.

As I was headed over the bridge tonight on my way home, I noticed that my fuel needle was bouncing off of the big E and looked like it was ready to stick at any minute. I usually get a little warning before that happens but I didn't get that this time. It seemed to happen rather suddenly, but whatever the case, I knew I had to get off the road ASAP and get to a gas station. As I know the area, I knew where I could find one, so I exited the road, made a couple of turns and rolled into the station to fill up.

While I was filling my tank, I noticed an elderly gentleman showing a slip of paper to the gas station attendant who was locked behind bulletproof glass and was of no help whatsoever. So the man with the paper glanced in my direction and then headed straight for me.

"Could you help me please, sir?"

"Sure—I can try. What's going on?"

"Do you know where Blossom Street is?"

"Here or in Boston?"

"In Boston."

"By the hospital?"

"Yes! But not the hospital. We're staying in a hotel on Blossom Street...by the hospital."

"Sure. I know right where it is. Give me a second to think of how to get you there."

So I thought it through and then started to explain it to him. He stopped me and asked me if I would explain it to his daughter over in the truck. So, I walked over and talked her through it. Every light, every turn, even the street names. I had it all, and she was writing it down on a little pad as I went. But the further I got into it, the more unsettled the man seemed to become.

After the second time through he stopped me and said, "How much would you charge me to take me there? Just lead the way in your car and let me follow."

(I felt the blood drain from my face. Now?? I just came from there!)

"Awh, nothin'. I'm not gonna take your money. But seriously, those directions will take you right there. They can't miss."

"I'll give you...$50.00 right now."

(I gotta be honest; I thought about it.) But I said, "No, put your money away. Where are you here from?"

"Northern Maine. Almost to Canada."

This guy had just come a LONG way and he appeared to be at the end of his rope. He had had enough and he needed to get to a hotel across the street from one of the finest hospitals in the country. The kind of hospital where they do things that they don't do in Northern Maine—or most anywhere for that matter. He sounded like a man who had just had the last straw loaded onto his back, but he was "old school" and he wasn't going to let it show.

There was no way I wasn't taking him. There really was nothing to decide. I told him to stay on my tail and I would get him there. So we pulled out of the parking lot and headed back toward the bridge.

But there was something funny about the trip back into the city. Something I hadn't ever seen before. We hit almost no traffic all the way in. Including on three roads that are notoriously heavy. We just cruised. All the way to Blossom St. and the hotel where he was staying. We hit every green light and we took the one exit that nobody else was taking. It was just as smooth as it could be. Almost like it was planned or something. Weird....

So when we got to where we were going, I jumped out in front of the hotel to be sure that he was where he wanted to be, and he jumped out of his truck with a smile on his face, and I swear, the faintest beginnings of tears in his eyes. He thanked me again and told me how much he appreciated it. The tears, if they were there at all, were clearly not about what I did, but about what he had been through to get there and probably even more about the reason that he was there in the first place. I never asked about it. Then he went into his wallet again and pulled out $40.00 and offered it to me. I told him that I couldn't take it, so he put one of the twenties away and held the other one out in front of me.

I said, "Really, it's OK. It was my pleasure."

But he wasn't having it. He just stood there in front of me holding that $20.00 out. He wouldn't put it away. It seemed to be somehow important to him that I take it. And I could hear his daughter, who was still in the truck, telling me to take somebody out to dinner with it or go to a movie or whatever else. But the old man just stood there, holding that bill out in front of him.

I said, "Ya know, you really don't need to." But what he said next is what changed it for me.

He said, "You don't know what I've been through."

I said, "Partner, yes I do. This is an easy town to get turned around in!"

We both laughed, I patted him on the shoulder and then I took his money. I didn't want to take it, but I did. It seemed important to him that I take it. Whether it was to even the ledger or to reimburse me for my trouble, or simply to validate his thanks. In any case it felt like the right thing to do, even though I was still uncomfortable with it. I think I'll just find a way to pay it forward.

Having been through some of this stuff with my own father, I felt like I recognized some of what I was seeing. The beginnings of a long journey. The look of uncertainty, insecurity, and even fear, thinly veiled behind a look of determination to hold it all together in spite of everything. Because that is what men of that generation do.

What I want to give back to him now (and this will just be our little secret), is to have everyone who reads this, take just a moment to either pray, or think, or meditate, or do whatever it is that you do, on behalf of this old man and his daughter. Two uncertain, insecure people, staying in a hotel across the street from the hospital, a long way from home.

▲ ▶ ▼ ▲ ▶ ▼ ▲ ▶ ▼ ▲ ▶ ▼ ▲ ▶ ▼ ▲ ▶ ▼ ▲ ▶ *Change*

I saw quite a thing today.

My work travels took me to the site of a recently decommissioned coal- and oil-fired power plant.

The plant had been decommissioned with the intention of replacing it with a newer, cleaner, and more efficient power plant. Better for the environment, safer, cheaper to run and maintain, with decades of good use ahead of it. But like every change, regardless of how much for the better, it was not without its casualties.

As I went in through the main door I was awestruck by what I saw, and moreover, by what I didn't see. The place was almost completely deserted. The last of the waste product, machinery, and anything salvageable had been all but removed. So there was no activity at all. No sounds and no movement within the plant.

Giant boilers and piping and tanks and vents sat motionless and silent. I noticed catwalks across the whole plant, two stories off the ground, with nobody on them. Offices unoccupied with no lights, and doors closed and locked. Signs posted around the plant, which warned of danger, high voltage, protective equipment required, and extreme hazard, stood as sentries, warning workmen who were no longer there of dangers that no longer existed.

I went through all kinds of security screening when I arrived, and after passing through, I met our guys on site. As I got my rig ready to load the last of the waste to be removed from the plant, the foreman came up to us and said, "I'm sorry guys, our fork drivers have all gone home."

"Home? It's only 1:30."

"I know. They've given up. There's nothing to do here."

"I'm not following. Do they work today?"

"Oh yeah. They were here this morning, but...they just left. About a half hour before you got here."

"Are they coming back?"

"Not today. They might be back tomorrow. Or, they might not. I really don't know."

As we talked a bit, he explained that the decommissioning of the plant had been going on for a couple of years and that as each stage was completed, workers had to be laid off. Over time, it amounted to hundreds of people. Those workers who held jobs vital to the operation of the plant were retained, until the next phase was completed and then they, in turn, were laid off. It went on like that in waves until about two weeks ago.

When I showed up today, the foreman told me that they were down to a skeleton crew of twelve. Twelve people. Twelve people were all that were left, in a plant that once employed thousands, and based on what I saw, I'm not sure why they even kept those twelve. There was literally nothing going on there. The place was a ghost town.

People who had spent their entire careers in that place were now out of a job. Some of them were young enough to start over. Some of them were old enough to call it a day and take an early retirement. But some of them, like several of them in the last two waves of layoffs, were right in that no-man's land. Middle-late fifties to early sixties. Too long in the tooth to start over, but not close enough to retirement to call it quits. Those folks were in a tough spot, and they knew it. And now they're discouraged, disillusioned, and in some cases, defeated. Like the guys who were supposed to be there today to load my truck. They just went home. They apparently either couldn't see the point in coming back, or just couldn't muster the energy to walk into that place, looking like it did, on a Friday afternoon.

The guy I was dealing with today loosened up a little as I told him not to worry about the fork drivers. I told him we'd take the stuff we could load by hand and come back for the big stuff later this week. No worries.

He appreciated it, thanked me and then took his hard hat off. He wiped the sweat of his brow with his shirt sleeve and said, "Man, this has been a tough year. I had to lay off the last two batches of guys, and I've known some of them for over 20 years. These guys weren't just my crew—they were my friends."

I asked him, "Can they get jobs when the new plant is built?"

"Yeah, some of 'em. But a lot of these guys are specialized. They spent their whole lives doing something here that won't transition to the next place because the equipment is obsolete. They don't even use it anymore. I don't know what some of these guys are going to do. They've worked here all their lives."

"Oh Lord...."

"I had a guy come to me a couple of months ago to talk about all of this and he was scared to death. He said that he has a daughter just finishing up her freshman year in college and a son who is a junior in high school who also wants to go to college. He has no idea of what he's going to do now. I felt sick about it, but what could I tell him?"

"Are there any other plants like this where they could go to work?"

"Not really. They're phasing them all out. When they get the new one built, it will take them about 15 minutes to get it up and running. The new stuff is just way better. Change isn't always easy I guess...."

"No, I promise you it's not. Been through plenty myself."

"If you hear of anything—anything at all, give me a call, will ya? These guys are really dependable, hard workers. They'll do just about anything."

"I absolutely will. I'm just not sure of what kinds of jobs are out there that they would be suited for, ya know?"

"Believe me, I know. They do too. But just run it by me. If you hear of anything."

So, I took his number, put it in my phone and climbed back up into my rig. I slowly pulled out of the staging area and rolled past the entrance to the empty lobby of the building on my right, with the weeds growing up around the front walk; the empty, cracked loading docks with the doors shut tight; and the fence on my left that that listed away and ran the length of the plant to the gate leading out. I said a little prayer for the guys who spent their lives in that place and who are trying to find a new place in this brave, cleaner, more efficient world.

I've been there.

▼▲ ▶ ▼▲ ▶ ▼▲ ▶ ▼▲ ▶ ▼▲ ▶ ▼▲ ▶ ▼▲ ▶ *FedEx*

I recently gave notice to my manager at FedEx that I was leaving to pursue another opportunity. However, I did so with no small regret. That company, started 40 years ago by a maverick with the constitution of a riverboat gambler, gave me an opportunity that no other company I know of would have, and for that I will always be loyal to it, and very, very grateful.

For me, leaving a job means leaving people, and I don't leave people easily because I don't take my friendships lightly, whether long or short. I guess there's no particular right or wrong in that. That's just me. I take friendships as deep as my friends are willing to take them, but due to the nature of our work and our busy lives, we do what we can with what we have and we build from there.

While working in another capacity at FedEx, I applied for an open position to drive tractor-trailers and, against all odds, I got it. I am deeply grateful to my two trainers, both of whom had the patience of Job with me and demanded professionalism in a job where it is sometimes sorely lacking.

One of them quiet, reflective, and spiritual, whose constant reminder to me when I was about to blow a gasket in frustration was, "Namaste...breathe." I've never seen such patience in an instructor. In anybody, really. He never got frustrated with me, or at least if he did, he never showed it. He made it fun. He constantly reinforced the importance of safety and of doing things the right way. No short cuts. To my surprise, he also let it slip one day that he was an alternate on the 1980 Olympic hockey team. The "Do you believe in miracles team." The team that books and movies have been written about. Missed it by one spot. He wasn't bragging about it when he told me. He just mentioned it in passing as part of a conversation we were having. He is universally loved and respected in that company. He has been there almost 30 years.

My other trainer, another longtime employee, was an intense man and a task master. He demanded that I do it right, all the time, and let me know when I didn't. He was never mean but he took the tack of a football coach. Something with which I was vaguely familiar. His methods made even more sense to me after I came to learn something of his childhood. The youngest of several children, he was put to work on his father's fishing boat at the age of seven. His father would roll him out of bed at three o'clock in the morning and they would stay out until well after dark, hauling in lines and working in all kinds of weather. By the age of 12, he could do everything.

He said, "There were no sick days on my dad's boat. Once we left shore, we weren't going back for anything. You ate while you worked, and if you were sick, you were sick while you worked." This was seven days a week, all summer, and every holiday until he left home. Blistering hot summer days, cold, rainy days, and everything in between.

He said that starting his day at FedEx at 2:00 a.m. and pulling three ton freight containers around a warehouse to load onto his rig for delivery is the easiest job he ever had. He still comes in to work on one of his days off because more than one day of rest is too much. He is fanatically detail oriented and is one of those guys who knows what needs to happen next before anybody else does. And contrary to what one might think based on this description, he is also hilariously funny.

I'll miss the hard edge and funny stories of a guy who grew up in the projects of South Boston. An Irish kid who joined the Marine Corps at 17, who once told me that Whitey Bulger (on whom the character of Frank Costello from the movie "The Departed" was based), used to buy him and his friends ice cream cones when they were kids. He told me several stories of that neighborhood in that time, some hilarious and some spine-tingling. He saw things and knew things that only a local kid would, and they were fascinating. I could talk to him for hours and never get it all.

I'll miss my wheelin'-dealin' buddy who is the go-to guy for anything you could possibly want. He owns a consignment shop in Boston as a side job. He is Red Redding from The Shawshank Redemption. Always moving, always working an angle, and always fun to be around. He always had a smile and was always cutting up with somebody. More times than I can remember, I would see somebody come up to him and say, "Hey, you got that thing I was asking about yet?" And I'd hear him say, "Yep —comin' in tomorrow. You want two?"

I'll miss my buddy who works at another station now, who emigrated from Puerto Rico a couple of years ago.

An extremely hard, conscientious, worker who speaks broken English and overcame the loss of two babies while living in poverty. He never showed weakness or sadness, even though I know he felt it. He is deeply grateful for his job and I am deeply grateful to have met him. He is another guy who was always fun to work with. He always had a positive attitude and was eager to learn everything he could—including English. A lot of nights we would trade off English lessons for Spanish lessons. We had a blast.

I'll miss seeing my little buddy, Casey, a single mother who works harder than any woman I've ever met. In fact she works harder than most of the men I've met. That woman never stopped moving from the time she punched in until the time she punched out. I'll miss the eye roll she would give me when I would plead with her to drop a box that was twice her weight, and then load it into a container that weighed more than her car, only to watch her try to pull the thing across the warehouse by herself. She is tall and might be a buck twenty soaking wet. The baby of five children, she learned this work ethic from her mother, who raised her, as her father died nine days after she was born. She honed this work ethic out of necessity when she took physical jobs normally reserved for brawny men.

But during the entire time I worked with her she always maintained a great sense of humor. A very pretty woman, she endured years of being hit on and harassed by the men with whom she worked (most of it intended to be playful), and managed to send all of them down in flames without offending them. That's not easy to do, by the way. That takes a lot of skill and tact. She told me once, "Tim, if I didn't know how to handle these guys, I would had to have quit years ago." A lot of those guys have come and gone. She's still there.

I'll miss my part time comrades, every one of whom is holding down two jobs to make ends meet. One of them owns and operates a big landscaping company, one is a master mechanic and auto body guy, and the other two are truck drivers for other another company. They always showed up for their shifts at 5:00 a.m. and then would head to their second jobs as soon as they punched out. Burning the candles at both ends, these guys are machines.

It would probably sound better to say that they never complained, but the fact is they complained all the time. We all did and it was hilarious. It's a big part of what made the job fun. I'll miss our crucially important, impromptu, meetings where we would plot the overthrow of the company. We always had it all figured out but never did anything. Usually, about the time we would get on a roll, one of us would look at the clock and realize that we had to get to work. The overthrow is still a work in progress.

I'll miss the guys who I trained with. The guys who were off and on as frustrated as I was, but who all overcame the challenges and moved through the process. My buddies, Jeff, Richie, and Robert (Dippy), who struggled along with me to learn this craft, and who beat me for a dozen jelly donuts in a training competition that I still think was rigged. There were times in our training when we weren't sure that we were going to ever get it. But we all made it through and we all received our Class A licenses.

I'll miss my manager, who is without question one of the best managers I have ever worked for. He held a tough line, but was always fair. I never once saw him compromise, but I also never saw him fail to make an effort to accommodate if he could. He had this terrific, dry sense of humor, but he always played along with mine—which wasn't so dry. He is a consummate professional with a college degree in engineering. He was fanatical about detail, about doing things right and about being safe. He also knew how to manage all of the different personality types with whom he worked. He was one of the best I've ever seen at it.

I'll miss the other full time guys, and the two sweetest girls in the office, Kate and Tracy, who covered and corrected my many paperwork mistakes and never said a word about it. I'll miss the pace, and the noise, and the fights, and the yelling, and the experienced guys offering me tips on how to do something better. They always had patience with me and they all told me, "Give yourself some time. This doesn't come overnight. We've all been there."

It wasn't without its drawbacks, but I can honestly say that this job was one of the most enjoyable jobs I've ever had, and the people there made it that way.

I will truly miss this place.

▷▼▲ ▷▼▲ ▷▼▲ ▷▼▲ ▷▼▲ ▷ GPS Detour

I don't really know where I am. I know *about* where I am, but I haven't taken a close look at a map since I got here, and I definitely don't know where anything else is. The perfect qualifications for a driver. Today's run took me through the hills of southeastern Pennsylvania into West Virginia, into Maryland, and back into West Virginia, where I stopped at the hospital in the metropolis of Keyser.

I didn't really trust my GPS to get me there, as once in a while she would get confused, but I didn't have a road map and the Google step-by-step directions were already on page two before I got out of the parking lot. So I scrapped that idea and decided to trust her. In her defense, she did seem to know where the place was that I needed to go, so I followed every turn and eventually ended up where I needed to be. I did my work at the hospital, grabbed some lunch, and punched in my return address to get back.

But this time she directed me to take different roads from the ones we took to get there. I already didn't completely trust her, as it took me about 45 minutes longer to get there than it was supposed to. So I turned her off, reprogrammed the destination and hit go...again. Same thing. Different roads. So now, I start talking back to her while I'm driving.

"In 100 feet...turn right on route 219...North."

"What?? WHY?! We didn't go that way before!!"

"Turn right...."

"I am telling you right now—you lead me on one of your little wild goose chases again, and you're goin' out the window!"

"Turn right...."

So I did. I turned right just to spite her. I knew she was wrong and I was going to prove it. And it went like this for three hours. She would tell me to turn and I would turn. I'd just say, "Fine. You want me to turn, I'll turn. And then when we get lost, I am going to sell you to pay for the hotel room that we're going to need!" Just as I suspected, we were WAY off the beaten path in no time. Fortunately, I had some time and I really don't mind driving, so I just settled into it and gave her the silent treatment. Long stretches of road with neither of us speaking a word.

And on this new path, we traversed back roads through hills and trees and burgs and beautiful little places that probably aren't even on the map. I saw rivers and little brooks. I saw a beaver dam and an old barn with a giant chipped and faded American flag painted on the side. I saw farm houses, grain silos, and fields that went forever. I crested two mountains and passed a sign that proudly said "The Eastern Continental Divide." Elevation 2800 ft.

I saw a hawk pacing my truck overhead, a couple of snow flurries, an Amish horse and buggy, and a baby goat prancing circles in a pen around its mother outside a farmhouse. I saw the evidence of a forest fire on dead trees by the side of the road, and I saw dozens, maybe scores, of houses in little villages, in disrepair, with cars up on blocks in the yards and sitting on acres of barren land.

One particular thing that struck me, and I'm not sure why, was a child's plastic toy car—the kind they sit in with the little plastic roof and then propel it with their feet—sitting alone, way out in a field. I wondered how it got that far from the house and why it was still there. I wondered if the baby it belonged to missed it, or even knew where it was.

I passed a feed store in a small town called Berlin, where I saw a little boy "helping" his dad lift a sack of feed into the back of a pickup truck. I passed a large property with the steel framework of a huge structure on it. The sign in front said, "Building Noah's Ark." It appeared to be quite an undertaking, and if they ever get it finished, it should be very impressive. I passed men burning trash in their front yards and saw a trailer off to the side of the road with a sign on the front door that said, "Enter At Own Risk." I passed a "Speedy Meedy" convenience store and some mom-and-pop diners that didn't even have a name.

I was so far out in the sticks that I couldn't get a radio station or a cell signal. When I did pick up a station, it was either the admonitions of a radio evangelist or "The Region's Best Country."

I was really enjoying the ride, and about the time that I was looking forward to the next thing on a detour that I didn't want to take in the first place, my girl piped up from the seat beside me and said, "In .9 miles...take ramp...on right...to Interstate 76...West."

And it dawned on me. I'd been had. She so did that on purpose. That whole detour was planned before we ever left.

I kind of looked at her, sheepishly, out of the corner of my eye, but she just kept looking straight ahead...trying to hide a smile.

I said, "You did that on purpose, didn't you?"

She said, "In .1 miles...take ramp...on right...to Interstate 76...West."

You see, I didn't want to be off of the big comfy main highway that I knew would take me where I wanted to go. It was flat, straight, and easy to navigate. And I didn't want that detour because I didn't know where it would lead. I didn't know what I would encounter along the way. But because I listened to the voice and trusted it, I got to see things that I couldn't see from the highway. Truly beautiful things. Things that I may never see again. I can see a highway anytime. But seeing what I saw today required a detour that I hadn't planned.

I don't really know whether the detour substantially lengthened my return trip or not. What I do know is that sometimes you have to trust that little voice that's telling you to get off the main road, even when you don't want to. Sometimes that little voice is calling you, against your better judgment, to take a trip for which you will be forever grateful.

Sometimes that little voice knows exactly what it's doing.

▼▲ ▶ ▼▲ ▶ ▼▲ ▶ ▼▲ ▶ ▼▲ ▶ ▼▲ ▶ ▼▲ ▶ *Politics*

Last night I had the TV tuned to the political debate between Mitt Romney and Barack Obama when my son walked in and plopped down beside me. He didn't say anything, but just watched it with me for a few minutes. Then he broke the silence.

TJ: "Dad, those guys were just shaking hands and smiling at each other five minutes ago, and now they're totally dissing each other!"

Dad: "Welcome to politics, son."

TJ: "They're both just saying that the other guy doesn't know what he's doing."

Dad: "Welcome to politics, son."

TJ: "Is Romney wearing a red tie and Obama wearing a blue tie because of their parties?"

Dad: "No—they're wearing those ties because they both paid image consultants thousands of dollars to run a menagerie of ties past focus groups to see which ones 'they' liked best."

TJ: "You're kidding...."

Dad: "Nupe."

TJ: "So people are going to make up their minds about who to vote for because of this debate?"

Dad: "No—most people made up their minds before the campaign started."

TJ: "Then why are they having them?"

Dad: "Because they have to play to a group called Undecided Voters who somehow can't tell the difference between what these two guys stand for and what they want to do if they get elected."

TJ: "But they keep saying how they are so different."

Dad: "Yep."

TJ: "Do you think they're different?"

Dad: "Couldn't be more different."

TJ: "And there are people that can't see that?"

Dad: "Apparently."

TJ: "I'm goin' to bed."

Dad: "I'm right behind ya, buddy."

▼▲▶▼▲▶▼▲▶▼▲▶▼▲▶▼▲▶▼▲▶ *BFFs*

So, like today...I got to work with my BFF 20-some-things at work. It was totally fun, and like it didn't even like feel like work at all! I know, right?!

They were all like, "Hey, it's totally cool that we, like, get to work together today!"

And I'm all, "I know!! It's totally gonna be a blast!"

And they're all like, "I know, right?!"

Then Kristi, Kristy, Christy, and Christi, were like, "OK, so just meet us over there and we'll like totally get stuff ready for when you get there!"

And I'm like, "OK, cool!"

And they're like, "Totally."

So then, like, I cruise over there—I'm like, all, vroom vroom, and they're all like, "Hey, like what took you so long? Did you, like, get lost or whatever?"

And I'm like, "Uh, no. Like I can't just cruise my whip around anywhere like your Prius! This thing is like, totally giant! I mean, like, I'm so sure. Like I'm just gonna totally go on the little tiny roads and bang U-Turns in the middle of traffic. I mean, I wish! Like, wouldn't that be funny if I could just totally whip around like you do in that scooter? OMG!"

And they're all like, "OMG, that would be so hilarious!"

So then like, while they were working, they all started talking about what they did last night. And like they all went out around 10:00 p.m. and were all like, "This place is lame," and they were totally over it, so like they went to a couple of other places until they found a good one, and then they, like, totally closed the place down! They totally do this every night! OMG! And then they were all like, "So what did you do last night?"

And I was all, like, "I went to bed."

And they were all like, "Woot Woot! Spill it!"

And I was like, "No. I, like, actually went to bed. By myself. Then I slept."

And like, I totally heard crickets....

▶▼▲ ▶▼▲ ▶▼▲ ▶▼▲ ▶ Grocery Shopping

I hate going to the grocery store and having to listen to the fighting and name calling and near-fisticuffs-type of arguments that break out whenever I'm there. Not among the other shoppers, mind you, but between the little angel that sits on my right shoulder and the little devil that sits on my left, BOTH of whom are yelling in my ears about what to buy. Unfortunately, I am not one of those blessed souls who naturally gravitate toward healthy and nutritious foods. Oh no. I am one of the accursed who want to eat yummy food. All the time. And don't even waste your energy trying to explain to me that broccoli and cauliflower are yummy foods. No, they're not. Period.

But that said, I decided that today I would make an effort to do it right, and embark yet again on my own Quixotic pursuit of health through better nutrition.

I walked in the store and headed straight to the fruit and vegetable section. In my right ear I'm hearing, "YEAH! Way to go! That's it! Gonna get all healthy, 'n' stuff!! This stuff is so good for you, you're gonna love the way you feel in a couple of weeks!"

But in my left ear I'm getting, "Dude...what are you doing? You're NEVER gonna eat this. It always looks good going in the cart, but as soon as you get it home, you KNOW it's gonna be the absolute last thing you want, and it's just gonna go bad."

So now I have to get involved and I tell them to both just hush up or we're going back to the car and we're not getting any food at all! So they both hushed up for the moment, and the healthy stuff made the cart. Score one for the right side. The golden silence lasted until we got to the next aisle.

Left ear guy: "OK, now THIS is what I'm talking about! You can never have too many bags of these!!"

Right ear guy: "You are NOT getting those! They're death in a bag!"

Me: "Yeah, but they're yummy death...."

Left ear: "YEAH! SEE! Moron...."

Right ear: "You know better than this...."

Me: "All right all right! I'm not getting' em. You happy now?!"

Right ear: "Well...happier. Say, how 'bout some of those rice cake things?"

Me & left ear: "NO!!!!!"

Right ear: "Geeeze, OK, OK...."

And it went on like this for 15 aisles and I was in a peach of a mood the whole time. I swear shopping is exhausting for me.

The end result is, we all compromised a little. I did, in fact, have fruits and vegetables in my cart. Four or five different kinds. I even tried to get all the colors in. On the other hand, a box of sugar-coated death cereal might possibly have found its way into the basket as well, but let's not get bogged down in the details. The point is, our bodies are well-oiled machines. Veritable miracles of Creation or Evolution, however you see it, and they must be maintained.

However, our minds...yea...our very souls, require a certain amount of guilty food pleasure now and then, or we just become well-oiled, sad, pathetic, miracles. Or at least that's what would happen to me, and I'll not have it, I tell you! I won't! I'm gonna be a happy miracle! But I'll try to eat enough of the sad food to allow me to keep eating the happy food every now and then.

▶▼▲▶▼▲▶▼▲▶▼▲▶ *Little White Cane*

Warm weather and sunshine tends to put a skip in the step of the hearty folks who endure New England winters, and yesterday, as I was out doing my thing, I saw it in full swing.

I saw a kid in his late teens bopping down the sidewalk, arms flailing, and rapping about I don't know what. But he was doing it, with a ball cap cocked to the side, flat brim and a huge smile. He was into it, and he didn't care who was watching.

I saw an elderly gentleman, had to be in his eighties or nineties, look at a young woman, smile, and touch the brim of his fedora as he passed her. I thought that stuff only happened in old movies, but I was wrong. Apparently, it also happens in the late spring on city streets in Boston when the sun is shining and the temps are above 60. For the record, she smiled back at him and nodded.

But the best thing I saw, the thing that left the biggest impression today, was the sight of a little girl, maybe nine or ten years old, skipping down the sidewalk as she held her mother's hand. She was smiling from ear to ear, talking non-stop, and clearly having a ball. By itself, that made me smile. But what really left the impression on me was that she was wearing sunglasses and sweeping the sidewalk in front of her with a white cane that she was holding in her free hand. This little girl was enjoying every minute of her day and her mother seemed to be enjoying it as much as she was.

And for the whole rest of the day and most of this one, I've been thinking about that little girl and wondering if she would believe me if I told her that I've been through too much to still be happy enough to skip and smile and just enjoy the sunshine.

I'm betting she wouldn't buy it.

▲ ▶ ▼ ▲ ▶ ▼ ▲ ▶ ▼ ▲ ▶ ▼ ▲ ▶ ▼ ▲ ▶ ▼ ▲ ▶   *NYC*

I'd have to say that the six scariest words that come out of the mouths of the managers and directors at my company are, "There's been a change in plans."

See, I was supposed to spend this week makin' some easy money shuttling loads between Queens, NY and a small town about 30 miles southeast of Pittsburgh, PA. Wide open highways, change of scenery, and for me, a chance to breathe. And then this morning, I heard, "There's been a change in plans." Followed by, "You and Dave will be together today. He'll show you what you're doing."

OK—no big problem. I'm nothing if not flexible. So I asked Dave, "Dave," I asked, "Are we headed to some little burg upstate? Maybe some charming little town somewhere in the Hudson Valley?"

Dave informed me that that was not the plan. The plan was to navigate my rig out of Queens, over the Triboro Bridge, down through Harlem, and right smack into Midtown Manhattan.

For the record, this is not my idea of easy money. If you've driven through Manhattan, at rush hour, while it's under construction—you're feelin' me. If you haven't—trust me, it's an adventure.

After an hour or so of some pretty fancy country driving, I found myself in the belly of the beast and eventually on site at Memorial Sloan Kettering Cancer center—a massive and world-famous institution where the staff does the work of the angels, and do it every day of the year.

I spent most of my time outside of the loading dock on the street, moving things off of and onto my truck. And that's where I got to witness what makes New York City, New York City.

The city is a caricature of itself. 6:30 a.m. and the first thing I heard after I got out of my truck were two other truck drivers across the street "F-Bombing" each other over one thing or another, full on, yelling at the tops of their lungs. I kind of laughed to myself when I heard it. I thought, "These guys are right out of central casting." And then as the rush hour became more congested, the friendly motorists started in with the horns. I've never heard such honking. I don't even know why they were honking. Nobody moved. It didn't change a single thing, but the honking seemed to make people feel better. Like they were actually affecting things for the positive.

I just stood there and took it all in. I saw a woman dressed in a business suit walking down the street carrying a briefcase. I saw a man walking down the street carrying a purse. I saw a kid, maybe 11 or 12 years old, walking down the street carrying a puppy. I saw a grizzled Vet in a camo jacket, sitting on a corner, carrying the weight of the world.

I must have been looking particularly "hot" in my hoodie and work boots, as a friendly young woman walked past me and smiled. Then she asked me if I was looking for a date. At 6:30 in the morning....

I thought it an odd time to be asked out, but, when I got it goin' on, I can be dangerous.

I politely declined as I explained to her that I was working, and didn't really bring the clothes for steppin' out anyway. It was a short conversation. She seemed to lose interest pretty quickly.

After we finished up, I slowly navigated my way out of the city and headed toward the metropolis of Jeanette, PA., about 30 miles southeast of Pittsburgh. I LOVE traveling through Pennsylvania. Dairy farms as far as the eye can see, with a few small mountains here and there. But mostly wide open space. More to my liking. And when I finally rolled into Jeannette, and arrived at my offload site, I met up with the same crew that was there before.

Big Nick, Little Nick (not making that up), Jeremy (Worm), and Tommy the new guy. These guys are as good as they get. Hard working, decent guys. The bluest of the blue collars. They work in a processing plant, emptying and washing medical waste bins. All day long. That's what they do. Then they load them back onto the trucks that brought them in. And they don't complain. They just do their thing. They always have a smile or a joke, and a little spring in their step. They're working for peanuts, but it's all relative. Out in that little Ampipe of a town, you can live on peanuts. They just get it done. Great guys, those four. I look forward to seeing them again.

The next day, I was scheduled to be back in Gotham. My GPS had a major brain fart on the way in and decided that rather than having me loop around the city and exiting into Queens, the best way for me and my rig to get to Queens was to take the Lincoln Tunnel and navigate my way through Manhattan and Harlem. During rush hour. I came very close to throwing it out the window. We ended up on 5th Ave., Park Ave., and Madison Ave. I drove past what looked like Rockefeller Center, Central Park, and about 40 million honking and swerving taxis. But, since my stop was in the city anyway, I found my way to where I was going, parked, and proceeded with a well-deserved, mini nervous breakdown. I got over it pretty quick.

But when the week was all said and done, I was instructed to park my truck back at our facility in Astoria, as I would be flying home so that they could use the truck for the upcoming week. And shortly after that is when I met the highlight of my trip. I was set up with a cab to take me to JFK airport, and it was waiting for me when I got out of my truck.

My driver was a young African. He told me, during the course of our conversation, that he was from Guinea, in West Africa, and that he had been here for seven years. I asked him if he lived in Queens and he said, no, "I live in the Bronx."

"Oh yeah, I drove past that. What brought you here?"

"I was entered into a lottery for a Green Card. It's part of a diversity program for Africans that the United States has. There are 50,000 spots and I got one."

"Well that's great! Congratulations! Do you like it here?"

"I love it. I got a job right away and I have already earned a Bachelor's degree."

(NOW this kid has my attention.)

"You're kidding.... What's your degree in?"

"Finance."

"No way. That's terrific! Do you plan to find work in finance?"

"I just did. I start my first professional job on Monday, with Dannon, as a financial analyst."

"Dude, you just made my day. In fact, you just made my whole week."

"I plan to work for two years to save some money, and then I want to get an MBA. Then I will get CFA. My dream is to someday own a house."

"So, why did you want to come to the U.S.?" (I already knew the answer, but I wanted to hear him say it.)

"Opportunity. In this country, if you are willing to work hard, you can make it. You can do anything."

"God bless you for saying that. A lot of people born and raised here don't seem to think so anymore."

"I don't think that. A lot of people want to blame other people for their misfortune. It makes them feel better. But they don't want to work. They should just look at themselves. Blaming somebody else doesn't help you."

"Man, you are so right."

"America is the greatest country in the world. She gave me a chance for a better life."

I literally had to swallow hard to keep from tearing up.

After the week I just spent in NYC, and in rural, Podunk, PA., and after my ride to JFK in the back of his taxi .... I think he may be right.

In fact—I'm pretty sure of it.

▼ ▲ ▶ ▼ ▲ ▶ *A Moment within a Moment*

Twelve years ago today, on 9/11, I had a "moment within a moment." I was shocked and angered like everyone else by the events of that awful day, but I was also concerned about a newfound friend of mine. His name was Mohammad, and he had a beautiful wife, two small children, and lived in a quiet neighborhood in southern New Hampshire. He was a devout Muslim of Lebanese descent and I wanted to check in with him to see how he was doing. I wanted to see how, and what, he was feeling, and if he and his family were all right.

The world had changed forever on that Tuesday morning, and nobody really knew what to expect next. I didn't really know what to expect from him either. I didn't know whether he would try to explain the attacks away, or perhaps become defensive and tell me that America had it coming. I wasn't going to ask, but I thought that it might come up in the course of the conversation. I mean—it had to, right? It was obvious. How was he going to get around it? It was the proverbial elephant in the room, and all I was going to do was open the door to the room and let him call it as he saw it.

So I called Mohammad and we talked for a while. He was somber, as was I, and didn't really have a whole lot to say. We talked about how tragic and senseless it was. We talked about what was to come next. Of course, neither of us knew, but we did know that this was only the beginning of a huge sea change in the country and perhaps in the world. I kept waiting for him to go where I thought he would go. I kept waiting for what "had" to come next. And then, finally, at the end of the conversation, it did. When we came to the end of the conversation and it was time to hang up, he thanked me for calling to check on him, and then he sighed deeply and said, "Tim, we're Americans. We'll get through this. We always do."

And that was the moment within the moment. Without realizing it, I had put my friend into a box. Fortunately, he didn't realize it either. But I had, in fact, done it. And at that very moment, he stepped out of that box, and he never went back into it again.

Sometimes the easiest thing to do is to put people in boxes. It's quick, efficient, and it keeps things tidy. But the problem with boxes is that they're only big enough to hold the stereotypes. They're never big enough to hold the people. I realized that day, that sometimes, despite appearances, the stereotype is wrong. Totally wrong. So on that day, I began tearing that box apart. And given all we have been through, it hasn't been an easy box for me to tear apart. But I will continue to tear at it. I will beat on it and rip it and pull down the sides, using any available tool I have. I don't want any more boxes.

▶▼▲ ▶▼▲ ▶▼▲ ▶▼▲ ▶▼▲ ▶▼▲ ▶▼▲ ▶ *Skip*

So I dropped in for a consult with a Harvard-trained ENT physician today to get a look at something that was nothing. Well, OK—something that is something, but that I can drastically affect with a moderate weight reduction of say, ten or fifty pounds.

For a while now, I am occasionally awakened at night by a loud noise in my bedroom, which sounds like a truck driver using a Jake Brake. (Look it up.) I have yet to find a truck in my room, so I surmised that I have literally been waking myself up with a ridiculously loud snore. As I determined that 2015 will be the year of Tim (at least from a health standpoint), I decided to get a referral from my PC guy and get it looked at.

When I arrived at the ENT office, I was met at the door by his lovely assistant, who asked me if I would like to slip into a spa robe and slippers, and offered me a sparkling water with fresh lemon slices while I waited. (This can't be good....) I politely declined and told her that I wouldn't need the hot towel either. So she smiled and directed me toward the desk, where I was handed what I thought was a copy of the Greater Boston phone book. It turned out to be the stack of medical forms that I was required to fill out before my appointment. I was then offered a seat in the massage chair to fill them out, and told to ring the little bell on the table next to it if I needed anything. I think I read the first one or two forms, but they all pretty much said the same thing. "If anything goes wrong, it's not our fault. If your insurance doesn't cover this (even if something goes wrong), you will pay for it."

So I quit reading after the second one and just started signing and then brought them back to the desk.

As I was finishing my fresh squeezed orange juice and small plate of papaya slices, I was called in for my consult. I could see that I was way underdressed for the occasion, but it was too late to do anything about it. I walked into the exam room, which smelled faintly of lavender, and took my seat in the heated leather recliner. I uttered a quick prayer about insurance coverage, which ended just as THE DOCTOR walked through the door. He was one of those guys who was blessed with Soap Opera good looks, and one of those perfect smiles where you see the little sparkle of light coming from a tooth and you hear the little "ting" that goes with it. He had on his white medical coat with the script writing above the left breast pocket that said:

"SKIP"
Ear Nose & Throat
Harvard Medical School

He introduced himself, as did I, and he sat down to look at my chart.

"Doc—I couldn't help noticing the name on your jacket. I was referred to a "Brian" something or other. Is that you?"

"Oh that.... Yes, I'm Brian. Skip is short for Skipper."

"Skipper?"

"Yes, I'm a yachting enthusiast."

(And I'm thinking, "Oh, of course you are... Do you also raise thoroughbreds??" Actually, I didn't want to know.)

"Well, I guess that explains the yachting magazines in the spa... sorry, waiting room."

"Guilty! Ha ha.... They're mine. Do you sail?"

"I've been on a few boats, but I don't 'sail' per se."

"Oh, you must try it. It's a divine way to spend a summer afternoon."

"Doc, I'm a truck driver. My summer afternoons are spent behind a wheel where I'll make as much in 14 hours as you've made since you walked into the room."

"I see. So what brings you in today?"

"Well, either somebody is driving a truck through my bedroom at night, or I have a snoring issue."

"Have you noticed any xerostomia or epistaxis?"

"Any what...??"

"Oh, sorry. Dry mouth or nose bleeds?"

"Yeah that's what I thought you said. Uh...no."

"I see—well let me take a look."

And so he did. He opened a drawer full of the most medieval-looking tools, and grabbers and stickers and probes, and he pulled out at least one of everything. I had things in my ears, in my mouth, down my throat, and best of all, a tube which he put in my nose and then sent down, about half way to my stomach. (I didn't even know a tube would do that.) Then I noticed that he had to move the latest issue of his yachting magazine to get to something else he wanted to insert. I didn't want anything else inserted, so I tried to distract him.

"Is that the latest issue, Doc?"

"Yes. Yes it is. Have you seen it? Here....Look at the center-fold on this one!" And he unfolded it for me to look at. "Isn't she magnificent?! My goodness, just look at that shape. And those lines. She just makes you want her somehow. "

"Uh...yeah. She's a beaut."

"I...uh...I don't just look at the pictures, you know! I subscribe for the articles."

"Oh, of course! Goes without saying."

He looked a little flushed, so he stuffed it quickly back into a drawer and then told me that I need surgery.

"Surgery?! For what?!"

"You have a deviated septum. It deviates to the right."

"No I don't."

"Yes you do. I don't even know how you're breathing right now."

"I'm breathing fine! I've never broken my nose, and I've never had a problem with it."

"Oh sure—that's what you say now. But you're not getting enough air."

"I'm getting plenty of air."

"But you could be getting more."

"I don't need more. I have plenty."

"No. You need more."

"Will it solve my snoring issue?"

"No, not by itself. But after I hook you up with a sleep study, a C-PAP, and a few follow-up visits, you'll be all set. But you need the surgery to be sure that you're getting all the air you can get."

"Yeah. Is that the whole deal, Doc?"

"Well...not the whole deal. I think you might be just slightly over your ideal weight."

"Doc—I'm a metric ton over my ideal weight."

"I was being diplomatic. If you get to your ideal weight, that will clear up most of this. But you still need more air. Should I go ahead and schedule the surgery?"

"Tell you what let's do.... Let me go through my house and clean out the happy food, and replace it with sad food, and then sit tight for a few months. How 'bout I lose the equivalent of a third grader, and then check back with you?"

"But...did you see the lines on that Palmer Johnson?"

"Yeah, she's quite something. How many more appointments do you have lined up today?"

"Five after lunch."

"You're gonna be fine. I'll see myself out."

"Can I call you?"

"How 'bout, I'll call you.... Happy Sailing, Skip."

▲ ▶ ▼ ▲ ▶ ▼ ▲ ▶ ▼ ▲ ▶ ▼ ▲ ▶ ▼ ▲ ▶ ▼ ▲ ▶ *The Exit*

I felt old when I woke up this morning. I worked hard yesterday, didn't get enough sleep last night, and I was feeling every bit of it. I was achy, tired, and highly unmotivated. But as I finally came to grips with the fact that it had to be done, I shut off my alarm, wiped the sleep out of my eyes and stumbled into the shower to get it all goin' again. After my shower and a cup o' Joe, I was awake and ready for a rare work trip to New York City. Well, not exactly the city, but not far from it. Astoria, to be exact— as I understand it, Astoria is part of Queens.

New York is a fascinating city. As a port of entry, it is inhabited by peoples from virtually every culture on the planet, who brought their respective cultures with them. Most of them didn't settle on the Upper East Side of Manhattan. They settled in working-class and lower-income sections of cities like the one I would be driving through today, and they put their respective stamps on those places. And today, I was particularly glad that they did, because I got to see it. You see, I grew up in Northern Colorado, which was not what you would call a giant melting pot, so a lot of this was new to me.

After being spun off of the interstate onto loops and bypasses, and then onto a main road, I closed in on my destination, which was the industrial section of town. As I turned off of the main road, I drove under a steel bridge where a subway passed overhead. Every car on it was tagged with graffiti, as was the bridge itself. Lined along either side of the narrow street were small shops with signs out front written in English, Arabic, Russian, Korean and a couple of languages I couldn't identify. One shop advertised sausage, pork, goat, lamb, kabob, and chicken, with slaughtered lambs hanging in the front window on display. I saw a cab driver arguing with a passenger, evidently over a fare, and two old women pushing a cart down the sidewalk, stopping every few feet to tap each other and wave their hands as they talked, while their headscarves blew in the breeze. I saw a young man on the sidewalk wearing a hoodie, sunglasses, and earbuds, furiously throwing punches and kicks at an adversary that only he could see.

The experience made me feel young again. It made me curious about the world and about this incredible city where so many came and settled and struggle to this day to make a life. I drove past the entrance to Rikers Island State Penitentiary, and under airliners on final approach to LaGuardia, no more than a hundred feet off the ground. I saw Yankee Stadium, a cathedral of a stadium surrounded by projects housing people who could hear the cheers from their stoops, but would never be able to afford to see a game there. I saw water, and bridges, tenements, and off in the distance, the Empire State Building, and the New Freedom Tower standing defiantly in place of the two that came before it. This city is exciting. It is alive, it is vibrant, and it makes you feel young. You really can't help it if you're not from here. It energizes you and it fills your senses. At least it did mine.

On the way out I took in everything I could see of New York, and then Connecticut as I headed back north towards Boston. I stopped at a truck stop along the way and chatted up the coffee angel behind the counter. She was cute, pleasant, and a little flirtatious. I enjoyed sparring with her and hearing her easy, infectious laugh. And I loved how she made me feel young again, too. And as I pulled out of that rest stop, I turned my radio on to resume my customary truck concert and I couldn't help thinking how much I was enjoying this trip.

But as I continued north, I drove past an exit sign that I had somehow missed on the other side of the freeway coming down. I'm not sure how I missed it then, but I did. But I didn't miss it coming back. The sign was clear and the directions were clear. The sign said, "Newtown—Sandy Hook." "Newtown" written above and "Sandy Hook" written below, with an arrow pointing off to the right. I wasn't ready for that. I slowed down a bit and looked over in the direction of where the road led. I'm sure it looked like every other small town in Connecticut did today, but somehow, to me, it didn't. It looked different over there. I was probably reading into it, but it somehow looked sad. It looked heavy. It looked grayer over there than it did anywhere else. The trees seemed to be more barren. The ground, colder. It left a strange heaviness on me.

I turned my radio off and passed the area as slowly and safely as I could, and I kept looking back on it until it wasn't safe to look anymore. I kept my radio off for miles after I passed that exit. Just didn't feel like singing. I just wanted to drive. So I did. And I thought about the kids. I thought about their parents, their friends, their families.

I thought about the school that will never again be used as a school and about all of the Christmas trees and decorations that came down 11 days before Christmas.

And I thought how I felt old again.

▼ ▲ ▶ ▼ ▲ ▶ ▼ ▲ ▶ ▼ ▲ ▶ ▼ ▲ ▶ ▼ ▲ ▶ ▼ ▲ ▶ *Friends*

I am certainly no preacher or Biblical scholar. (And all the people said, "Amen.") So the following account is not a Bible lesson. Not really, anyway. But it is an example of a time in which a Bible verse from my youth met up with a night in my life that I will never forget. Consequently, I'll probably never forget that verse again either.

In August of 2009, I went back to Colorado for my 30th high school reunion. I had never been to a reunion before, but, for whatever reason, I really wanted to go to this one. A lot of people were talking about it beforehand and it seemed like it had the potential to be a lot of fun. Plus, it would give me a chance to spend a few days with my parents, who I hadn't seen enough of in the preceding years anyway.

For a whole bundle of reasons, my life, in the preceding half dozen years or so, had not been a smooth ride. I had lost a job, a marriage, a lot of my faith, virtually all of my money, and my self-confidence. It was all gone. I was really struggling, and I was not in a good place.

In fact, I was in a dark and scary place. This was unfamiliar to me. I had always been an optimist. One of those guys who could always "find the pony in there somewhere." I had seen a lot of success in my life, and I had plans for more. I dreamed big and I set big goals. Most of the time I either hit them or came close enough to reach out and touch them. But during this long, unfamiliar stretch, I was in the washing machine and I couldn't find a way out of it. It seemed like one thing after another was coming at me and all I wanted to do was come up for air. If you've been through something like this, you know exactly what I'm talking about. If you haven't—trust me. It's bad and you don't want it.

I'm actually not really sure why I wanted to go to this thing. I certainly didn't have any success to brag about. I had lost touch with virtually everybody I went to school with, and had only recently reconnected with a few of my classmates on social media. But something kept pulling me there. Maybe it was just a desire to say hello to some old friends and see some familiar faces again. That, by itself, would have made the trip worth it for me. So I decided to go and made my way back to Colorado.

The night of the reunion I was excited and a little apprehensive. I wasn't sure of what to expect or of how I would be received. Honestly, but for the name tags they passed out with our class pictures on the front, I don't think anybody would have recognized me, and I probably wouldn't have recognized most of them either. But the reunion went beautifully. I reconnected with old friends, met some new ones, and laughed until my sides hurt. I can honestly say that it ranks in the top ten best days of my life. What happened that night triggered the beginning of a long awaited and badly needed change for me.

That night reminded me of who I once was, and who I might be again.

In high school, I was an athlete, a musician, an A/B student, and I had a lot of good friends. I wasn't really one of the popular kids, but I didn't really care to be. I knew all of them and I was friends with most of them, but I didn't fit the mold. I kind of did my own thing, and I looked forward to every day I was in that place.

But 30 years later, I found myself in a very different place. A place that I dreaded, where I was no longer an athlete or a musician. I didn't have a lot of good friends anymore, and popularity seemed to be reserved for those who had money or who stood high atop the corporate ladder. Successful, happy people were popular. I was neither. I was in a bad place and I couldn't find my way out of it.

So I say all of that to say this; do you know—I mean, really know—who your friends are? I found out that night, at least for me, that they are the people who are able to look past the façades that they see standing in front of them and really see us. They are the people who can look into our eyes, into our very souls, and make us recall that spark of Divinity within us and the dreams we once had. At one time or another, we all had them. And these people reach in and pull them back out. They remind us that once upon a time we brushed up against the success and happiness for which we were destined and that we might yet find again. They even make us believe that it might not even be as far away as it seems.

As adults now, we know that life can be very hard on dreams. Life can take those souls who at one time were so full of hope, curiosity, determination, confidence, and perseverance, and wear them down until they find themselves living in that wasteland where dreams go to die. Where disappointment and regret flourish like weeds in an abandoned lot. We can become worn down to where we *actually believe* that the divinity we once manifested was no more than a happy accident. It's an insidious process. It doesn't happen overnight. It can take years.

That night, the night of my reunion, I found out that our friends are those brave souls who won't allow us to remain in that dark place. That place from which the cynics, the doubters, the jaded, and the heartbroken, tell those of us who dare to hope for something more that there is no more. That this is just the way life is and that we would do well to make our peace with it. But our friends won't settle for that. They won't allow us to settle for it either. They beckon to the very best that was once in us. They remind us of who we were and had hoped to become, and they call it out.

That is exactly what they did for me on that August night in 2009. They looked into my eyes and they saw the 18-year-old kid standing in front of them. Full of life, full of potential, and full of possibility. They didn't see who I was that night. They saw was who I was 30 years ago, and who I could still be again. And then they made me see it.

My situation didn't change overnight. That almost never happens, even in the best of circumstances. But after being around them for a couple of days, the way I saw myself changed. I began to believe again that I still have the chance to fulfill my potential, whatever it may be, and in whatever way I choose. That it is never too late and that whatever was in me then is still in me now. It just needed to be reawakened and called forth.

And that night, the Bible verse from my youth came back to me. It is from the book of Proverbs, 23rd chapter, 9th verse and says, "As a man thinks in his heart, so is he."

To my dear friends who were with me that weekend, and to those of you who have encouraged me along the way, thank you. I'll never forget what you did for me.

▲ ▶ ▼ ▲ ▶ ▼ ▲ ▶ ▼ ▲ ▶ ▼ ▲ ▶ ▼ ▲ ▶ *Little Rocker*

I'll bet, not exaggerating, that I've seen a thousand of them in the years that I've been driving the highways and byways of this great country. Some of them in congested areas in or near cities, and some of them along lone stretches of empty highway, out in the middle of nowhere. They're not hard to spot. Markers set up along the side of the road, usually with a little cross, and maybe some ribbons attached. Some of them adorned with pictures or notes along with a wreath or flowers. Whatever they look like—however they've been decorated—they're all set up to commemorate a death. Or more accurately, a life cut short. They always give me a moment's pause. Truthfully, not much more than that, but it always occurs to me that "there but by the grace of God go I."

Yesterday, as I coaxed my rig through the hills of Southern Vermont, I passed yet another one. Just off to the left side of the road, not 50 feet from the shoulder. As they all do, it caught my attention, but this one bothered me. I've been thinking about it for a day and a half and it won't leave me alone. It bothered me because this marker had a cross, a wreath, some flowers, and some light blue ribbons attached to it. However, beside the wreath, on the left side, was a tiny rocking chair with a teddy bear in it. One of those little rocking chairs that two and three-year-olds sit in to look at pop-up books and watch cartoons.

That marker was only in my field of vision for a few seconds, but I can't shake it. I can't shake the baby blue ribbons and the rocker and the teddy bear. Somebody lost a baby. Right there at that spot. A baby with a teddy bear and a little rocker and a whole life in front of him.

As I am wont to do on long trips when I can't get a decent radio station, I just started thinking. I thought about that baby and I wondered how old he was. I wondered what he looked like. What his parents were like. I wondered if he had any siblings or maybe a dog waiting for him at home. I wondered if he had seen enough of life to have ever been in a swimming pool, or played in the snow. Or ridden a pony at a carnival—both hands on the saddle horn in a white knuckle death grip.

I wondered if he had known the joy of running through the grass barefoot in the summertime or that of jumping into a pile of leaves in late October. I wondered what he dressed up as for Halloween last year. I wondered about how different his childhood was from mine, and at the same time, how similar. I wondered if his heart skipped a beat whenever he heard the ice cream truck coming down the street. I wondered if he liked drawing pictures in preschool. I wondered if he was asleep in the car in the last few seconds of his life.

Sometimes it's not good for people like me to have a lot of time to think. Sometimes people like me have to think about unpleasant things, and when we do, we have to think them all the way through. Not always. But sometimes. And sometimes the things we think lead us to ask very tough questions about our faith. Not always. But sometimes. And sometimes the things we think lead us to hope harder than ever that we're right about our faith. That little boys don't die by the side of the road with their lives unlived, but that they just get to live them out in a better, happier place. A place where cars don't crash and people don't lose babies and the ice cream is free.

I even wondered, on some level, if that little boy could have known that I was thinking about him. I wondered if he could have known that a mile up the road from his marker I was swallowing hard and blinking back tears. I wondered, whenever he sees my truck roll up and down that stretch of road, if he might possibly put in a good word for me. Maybe at ice cream time.

Not always. But sometimes.

▲ ▶ ▼ ▲ ▶ ▼ ▲ ▶ ▼ ▲ ▶ ▼ ▲ ▶ The Little Things

Rolling out of bed in the wee hours of the morning is never easy for me. But, in my case at least, it comes with the territory and I do it every day. I'm certainly not alone in this. A lot of us do it and we don't get medals for it. It's just what we do.

But today, I got a real treat. After I picked up my keys and orders for the day, I was making my way across the empty truck yard toward my awaiting princess when I was stopped in my tracks. I looked up and noticed the full moon setting in the west, then looked the other way and saw the eastern sky painted completely in pink and orange just ahead of the rising sun. It was a moment I'll probably never forget and for that moment, all of the things that weigh me down, the things that seem to stress me out and steal my joy so easily, just...vanished.

I'll bet I stood there for two or three full minutes and just let it sink in. I watched the moon fade slowly in the West, and I watched the eastern sky until the sun just broke the plane of the horizon. Once or twice, I even closed my eyes and breathed in the crisp fall air.

I'm really not one to do this sort of thing very often, and absolutely never if anybody else is around. But I think I might change that in the coming days. I need more of that. I need what it did for me. How it made me feel. It was one of those times when all of the "big important" things suddenly became very small, and the small things, that I all too often overlook, became very....very.... big.

The Old Man with the Squeegee

Today is of those December mornings in Boston that makes you turn your collar up and jam your hands down into your pockets as you walk down the street. The skies are overcast, spitting snow, with a breeze out of the North dropping the reported temps into the low 30s.

As I was making my way to my corner Dunkin' for my morning fill-up, my attention was drawn to a little old man who was outside washing the windows and whistling "Good King Wenceslas" as he worked. As I came up to him, I could see that he was taking his time. He was doing it right. He used his Squeegee for the big stuff, and then he would take a rag out of his pocket to wipe off any little mark that he had missed.

When he saw me he smiled, real big, and said good morning. I returned it and said, "How are ya today?"

He said, "Mighty fine, mighty fine—and you?"

I smiled. "Oh, I'm fine."

But I knew that I wasn't as fine as he was. I probably hadn't been in a long time. But I was happy for that little old man washing the windows in the December cold and whistling as he worked, and I was intrigued by him. That little old man knows something that I don't know. And it's keeping him warm.

▼ ▲ ▶ ▼ ▲ ▶ ▼ ▲ ▶ ▼ ▲ ▶ ▼ ▲ ▶ *Welcome Home*

I saw a reunion this morning, between two older gentlemen who had never met. It left an impression on me.

I pulled into a McDonald's for a coffee and as I was standing in the breakfast line, an older guy in front of me, probably in his sixties, stepped out of line and into the line beside us, tapped another similarly-aged guy on the shoulder, and said, "Welcome home."

The second guy turned to look at the first, and seemed momentarily confused. Then he smiled and said, "Thank you brother. Welcome home to you too."

The first guy said, "When were you there?"

"'68 to '71. How about you?"

"'67 to '70. Where were you?"

"Khe Sanh. You?"

"Just south of you. Da Nang."

"No kidding...."

They both just sort of stood there and looked at each other for a few seconds, probably stirring up memories they had spent decades packing away.

I stood there in kind of a stunned silence while people walked around them and biscuit angels hustled up food and people looked for sugar for their coffees. I hadn't noticed it until that moment, but both of them were wearing Viet Nam Veterans ball caps. Neither of them saw me standing there just behind them, and they didn't see me wave a guy around me in line. There were no tears or joyful hugs between them. Just a moment or two of pause as they looked at each other.

Something passed between those guys in that moment. A connection that only warriors with the common experience of battle really understand. And when it had passed, the first guy smiled again and said, "Welcome home brother."

The second guy smiled back and said, "Thank you, man. Really. Welcome home to you too."

It occurred to me later that these guys were part of the only generation of American soldiers who returned from the hell of war to a hostile reception from their own countrymen. They weren't welcomed home like the warriors of any war before or since. They were vilified. They were spat upon in airports as they disembarked the planes that brought them back. They were shunned and blamed and made to be scapegoats for things over which they had no control or hadn't even done. And far too many of them were lost.

The two guys I saw that day were part of that group, and I suspected, from what I saw in their eyes, that they may have experienced some of the same things.

They didn't get to pay for their coffees this morning as somebody in line took care of it for them. Not much of a gesture after four decades, but hopefully one that expressed to them that after all this time, we finally figured it out. They are part of us. And they are finally welcome home.

▶▼▲ ▶▼▲ ▶▼▲ ▶▼▲ ▶ *First One Through*

Some way or another, TJ and I were talking about funny football stories that we had each experienced, so I jumped into the Wayback Machine and told him about a time when I was in junior high (seventh, eighth and ninth grade for my East Coast friends), when we unintentionally pranked an eighth grade kid.

See, he was a little "round" kid whose life's ambition was to be the first guy through the ring that the cheerleaders made for us to run through when we came out of the locker room after half time. You see them all the time at high school football games. It's a steel ring, about seven feet or so in diameter, and it's covered with paper. Then the cheerleaders would paint some inspirational type message on it to help fire up the team and the crowd. (Worked every time.) "Mangle the Mustangs, Beat the Bears, Ravage the Rams," something real clever like that.

So, the first guy in line got to break the paper, and then the rest of the team would follow behind. The whole team ran through the ring. That was the rule.

So, I'm telling TJ the story of how this kid lingered by the door in the back of the locker room so that he could be the first one out. He never got to play, so he was going to get his ten seconds of glory some other way. At least for that year. As we made our way out, he stayed WAY in the back so that he would be at the front of the line going out onto the field. When we got to the field, our coach gave us a few final words and then turned us toward the ring. Then he said, "All right guys...one more thing."

But this kid didn't hear the "one more thing" part. He took off, at full, waddling speed, arms flapping at his sides, and broke through the ring. First one out. First one through. But the rest of us stayed right where we were, still listening to our coach, until we heard the paper tear. Then the team, the coach, the managers, and the cheerleaders, ALL looked at that one kid, who had just broken the paper...all by himself. And when he realized that he didn't hear footsteps and yelling behind him, he stopped in his tracks, then turned around and looked at us. We couldn't help ourselves. We were doubled over, laughing. And he just stood there staring at us through what was left of the paper on that ring.

TJ was howling, and I was laughing just remembering the sight of it. It was genuinely funny, but looking back at it now, as an adult, I can see it probably remains a memory for that kid that he would rather forget. And as T and I were laughing about it, I grabbed my yearbook from the ninth grade to show him a picture of the kid. That made him laugh even harder.

Then, the paradigm shift happened.

We flipped a page and the pictures of the individual kids came up. Rows of 14- and 15-year-old kids, with their whole lives ahead of them. He pointed at one picture and asked me who it was. I said, "He was a friend of mine then. Last I heard, he's working overseas in the oil business." Then the faces and the memories started jumping off the page.

"This kid was real popular in school. He got into a bad accident a few years ago and had some brain damage. He's had a tough time since then."

"This kid became an airline pilot. He died a year or two ago when he was putting a new private plane through its paces. They're not sure what went wrong, but it crashed."

"This kid was super popular. One of the nicest kids in the school. Everybody loved him. He always had a girlfriend. Turned out he was gay. He moved to San Francisco at some point and became an activist in the gay rights movement and in the fights against AIDS. They didn't even know what they were dealing with then. He contracted AIDS and died back in the 80s."

And I kept flipping the pages.

"This kid became mentally ill. Not sure what it was."

"This kid is doing time."

"This girl died."

"I had a crush on this one. And this one over here. And about a year later, this one too."

"These two were really good kids, and I heard that they both developed bad drug addictions. Not sure where they are now."

"Same with this one. I played sports with him for years. He's dead now."

"This girl was hilarious. She was as good as they got. We were really good friends. I heard that after high school, her mom married a guy with a lot of money and it completely changed her. The friends I had who still knew her said that they didn't even know her anymore."

"This kid was one of the best guitar players I ever heard. He was amazing. In high school, he would bring the house down during breaks at the basketball games. He played in the pep band. He played that thing all the time. I heard he doesn't play anymore."

"This kid is doing life in the State Pen."

"This girl had a crush on me, but I didn't know it. Then years later I had a crush on her but she didn't care." (T thought that was funny.)

"This kid is a minister, this one works in the oil fields in Texas, and this guy is a huge tycoon with a major company overseas. We always knew he was going to do something big."

Then I closed the book and put it back on the shelf. TJ said, "I wonder what I'll be saying about my friends in 40 years."

I said, "No tellin', buddy. But the way life goes, it will probably be pretty similar. Some will have done well for themselves, some will have had a long run of bad luck, and some won't be with us anymore. But do yourself a favor; try to keep up with as many of them as you can. Even if it's just once in a while. Your friends and family are really what make this ride worthwhile. There will always be other things to keep you busy and distract you, but at the end of the day, it's the people you don't forget. You always remember the people. Always."

▲ ▷ ▼ ▲ ▷ ▼ ▲ ▷ ▼ ▲ ▷ ▼ ▲ ▷ *Clean and Sober*

Last Friday I was dispatched to the V.A. in the middle of Boston to pick up a couple of small drums of empty Methadone vials, from the Methadone clinic up on the second floor of the building. It's a stop I've made several times before, and it's pretty uneventful. But there was an event on Friday. An extraordinarily uplifting and encouraging event, and for me, maybe a bit of a game changer.

As I was up in the clinic, replacing the full drums with the empties, and labeling them up for transport, a man walked in, deliberately—slowly—with the aid of a cane, and looked right at me and said, "Good Morning!"

"Well good morning to you too! How you doin'?"

"I'm great. I'm clean."

"No kidding? That's great! Good for you!"

"Yep. Been clean for almost a year now. My God that was a long road back...."

This guy had short cropped hair, clean clothes, and clear, piercing blue eyes. And he had a smile.

"Oh yeah? Man, that is great! I love hearing that!"

"Yeah, it is great. I'm still in a lot of pain, but I'm learning how to manage it better. Doin' it the right way too."

"Oh yeah?" Something about this guy just hooked me and reeled me in. I had to talk to him. I didn't have a choice. So I stopped what I was doing and asked him, "Chronic pain, or something that happened recently?"

"Oh...chronic. I've had it since I got back from Iraq."

(Now, I'm all in.)

"When were you there, brotha?"

"2002-2003."

"What happened?"

"The story you probably heard a hundred times on the news. I was in a Humvee and we rolled over an I.E.D. Blew me all to shit. I didn't lose anything, but it messed me up pretty good. They gave me a lot of pain pills to help me deal with the pain, and then I got addicted to them. Then I started smokin' dope to help the pain pills, then I got into other stuff...."

"That's easy to do, brotha. You sure ain't the only one."

"Yeah, I guess it is. It wasn't too long before I was homeless, and loaded on somethin' all the time. First it was to beat back the pain then it was to beat back the addiction."

"That had to have been hell...."

"You can't imagine how hard it is. You wake up in the morning still drunk from the day before, or two days or a week...it all runs together, and you stink, 'cuz you can't even remember the last time you had a shower. Your clothes stink, your hair is matted, and everything you own is in a shopping cart. The only thing you know to do is fold up the cardboard you slept on, grab your cart, if someone didn't steal it during the night, and then start movin'. You just start pushin' your cart and you don't even know where you're goin'."

"I'm guessing that having people glare at you as they walked by didn't help things either...."

"Nah. Most of 'em... just about all of 'em, wouldn't look at all. They walked by like you wasn't even there. I guess I don't blame 'em."

"And all you wanted was enough change for a coffee or a burger, right?"

"Ah hell no, man. We all wanted the same thing. We were all beatin' back something. If it wasn't pain, it was addiction, and if it wasn't that, it was just tryin' to escape for a few hours. It's a miserable life. Sometimes all you wanted was a little change, and sometimes all you wanted was to apologize. I'm sorry I'm homeless. I'm sorry I look like this. I'm sorry I stink. I'm sorry I got blown up and addicted to pain pills.... Ya know? My own mother wouldn't even talk to me for three years. We are just now starting to get it right again. She told me that from now on, she would support me. You have no idea how much that means. Just having somebody that cares about you. Aaaauugh. I don't wanna sound like a wuss...."

"Dude—you have no idea how inspiring this is to me. You climbed out of that, and now you're clean and sober?"

"Yep. I've been pissin' clean for almost a year. They keep tellin' me that my tests are comin' back clean."

"Where are you staying now?"

"Oh!! That's the best part!! I'm in this place, kinda like a halfway house. The V.A. pays for it as long as I stay clean! I got my own room! It has a big bed, and a bureau, and a shower!! Man, it's beautiful! I love it there!"

(If you know me, you know that I am biting my lip and swallowing hard about now.)

"Are you able to work or are you disabled?"

"Well, I can't do much 'cuz of this." He held up his cane. "But I want to work. I just have to find something I can do. I think I could still work though."

"What did you do before all of this?"

"I was a truck driver. I went coast to coast for a couple of years. I was pretty good at it too. Knew all the back roads in most of the states."

"Is your license still good?"

"Yessir. CDL Class A. Clean too."

"Brotha—I don't know if we have anything for you, but I want you to call this number, ask for this woman, and tell her you talked to me. We might not have anything, but you never know. I'll tell her we met and to expect your call."

"Man, thank you so much! I'll call her as soon as I'm done here!"

"What's your name, sir?"

"Sean. And yours?"

"Tim. It's been a real pleasure to meet you."

About that time, the guy came out from the back, called my boy and handed him his cup. I grabbed up my 30-gallon drums, one in each hand, and wrestled them down the hall and out the door to my truck.

I passed a couple of guys on the sidewalk outside the building, near my truck, who had clearly seen better days. One of them hit me up for a donation.

"I'm sorry sir, do you have any loose change you could spare?"

"You don't have to apologize to me. I don't have much, but I'll give you what I have." And I dropped whatever little bit I had on me into his cup.

"Thank you sir. God bless you."

I'll bet I've heard that phrase a thousand times in my life, and never heard it once. "I'm sorry sir...."

It means something different to me now. After Sean explained it to me, I don't think I'll ever hear it the same way again.

And I wanted to tell the guys there that I had just met a guy who had been where they are, not a year ago, and battled his way out of it. But how do you start into that conversation? How do you explain to a guy who is still half in the bag, matted, and rank, that there might be a way out? Maybe you can't. Maybe they have to find it themselves, like Sean did.

But at the same time, maybe having that little hope that somebody is pulling for them, even if it's just for a few seconds, can make a difference. I don't know. I really don't.

My guess is that the road to recovery is an awfully long walk behind a shopping cart which holds everything you own. But it can be done. I met a guy who did it.

A guy who wakes up every morning in his own room, in his own bed, with a big bureau and even a shower, that he can use any time he wants to. A guy who told me, "Every day I wake up in this bed, I thank God that I'm not still on the street."

So this week my company asked me for a favor, which entailed heading to a vacation resort town not far from Pittsburgh, PA., for the week, to support an operation that we just acquired. Today's travels took me to a small town in West Virginia where I met an old codger named Jimbo somethin' somethin'. He was every bit of 85 years old and he was hunched over at the waist, but he was still doing work. He was also sporting a Red Sox cap. That caught my attention, so I asked him about it. He kind of smiled and shrugged it off, and through a raspy, weak voice he said, "I used to play for them."

If you know me at all, you know that work was over at that moment.

I said, "Hold on, Jimbo. You played for them??"

"Well, I played in the minors for them. Never made it to the big leagues."

"I live in Boston now. Who did you play with that I might have heard of?"

"Well, I didn't play for the Red Sox. I played for the Boston Braves and the Brooklyn Dodgers."

The man had my attention.

"Who did you play with, Jimbo?"

"Well sir, I was in camp with Sandy Koufax, Roy Campanella, and Jackie Robinson."

"What was it like being in camp with Robinson? Was there racial tension? Was there a lot of press hype and all of that?"

"No, not really. It was no big deal. Robinson was a good fella and he worked hard. We didn't have any problem with him."

"No tension or people being on pins and needles around him?"

"No. I mean those were the days when they had colored water fountains and all of that CRAP!!"

It seemed to me that his calling it crap wasn't a recent feeling. I got the sense that he felt that way at the time, just by the way he told the story.

"Baseball is a lot different now, huh?"

"Oh yeah."

"Did you sign a multimillion dollar contract?"

He smiled and kind of laughed and said, "No sir, we didn't make any money in those days. If we ever went out after a practice or a game we would have to split a milkshake."

"You what?"

"Oh yeah, we didn't have enough money to get our own, so we would split one."

"How did you get into it? Did you get drafted?"

And then he told me a story right out of Field of Dreams.

"When I was a kid, I was pretty good, and one of the adults saw me play one time and took me down to a park where there was a bunch of 20- and 30-year-old men getting ready for a game. He told one of the guys there that if they didn't have enough players, this kid could play. They said that I was too young and I couldn't play, but as it got closer to game time, they were one short so this guy comes up to me and says, 'All right kid, you want to play?' And I said, 'I'll play if you want me to.' And so they found a uniform for me and put me in. I struck out the first three batters I faced and I think I only allowed a couple of hits that day, and then...I was on the team from that day on. That's how I got started."

My partner was starting to get a little impatient, and I could NOT have cared less, but Jimbo noticed it and said, "I've got to get back down the hall and see what they want me to do next. You gonna be back Wednesday to get the rest of this stuff?"

"I don't know, Jimbo. But I sure hope so."

So that was my Monday. The names and places were changed to protect the innocent, but every other part of it is an absolutely true story. Tomorrow I head south through Pennsylvania, Virginia, and into Maryland. I'm already wondering who I'll meet.

▶▼▲▶▼▲▶▼▲▶ *A Day Like Any Other*

The way she told it to me, it was just time for a change. A sweet young farm girl from Arkansas had moved to the big city of Memphis to work in a bank and begin a life there, but she wasn't satisfied. She decided it was time to see the world and do something exciting. Something outside of her comfort zone. She was adventurous and wanted to see the world outside of her native Southeast, so, somewhat on a whim, she applied for a job as a flight attendant with United Airlines, and got it.

She was hired in and after she completed her training in January of 2001, she was stationed in Boston, MA. She had met lots of people during her short time with the airline, and had made several new friends. All of them, like her, excited for the change, excited for the new career opportunity, and excited to begin the next chapter of their lives.

The sweet, young farm girl, whom I affectionately refer to as Lambkin, had logged thousands of air miles over the ensuing year. She spent quite a lot of that time flying coast to coast, Boston to San Francisco, Boston to Los Angeles, etc., and she was getting comfortable with her duties.

In early September of that year, after about nine months on the job, she was scheduled as a reserve flight attendant for the second Tuesday of the month, which meant that she would be available to substitute for a scheduled flight attendant who, for whatever reason, couldn't work that flight. However, she was also scheduled for an annual training in Chicago, shortly thereafter.

As it happened, she had a friend who was going to be in Chicago the week prior to her training, so she asked the powers that be if it would be all right to move her training week up by one week so that she could meet her friend for a visit. As one might imagine, scheduling hundreds of employees to cover and cross-cover their various assignments is a daunting task. But her managers said that they could accommodate her and that they would see her for training on the week that she requested. She told me that this almost never happens.

So the Tuesday that she was set to fly out to training, she took the shuttle to the airport and as she made her way to her gate, she passed several of her flight attendant friends and colleagues. She stopped at Gate 19 and exchanged greetings with a flight attendant that she had spoken with just the day before. She saw a few other familiar faces and a couple she hadn't met yet. (But she knew that with schedules the way they are, she would meet all of them one day soon.) One of the girls asked Lambkin if she had worked this flight before, and she told them that she had, many times. But today she wouldn't be on that flight because she was headed to Chicago for training.

As it was getting closer to her departure time, she said that she needed to get going down to her departure gate, which was Gate 17. Just two gates away. She smiled and waved and told them that she would let them get back to their conversations. Normal conversations, I suspect. Conversations about traffic, about new boyfriends, about which flights were the good ones and who had vacation time coming. Maybe even a conversation about where they would eat that night when they got into Los Angeles. In every way, the day was shaping up to be a day like any other. It was a beautiful, sunny, Tuesday morning, September 11, 2001. They enjoyed their conversations over Styrofoam cups of coffee, as they awaited their call to board Flight 175 to begin their work day.

The crew consisted of two pilots and six flight attendants. In all, they welcomed 56 passengers aboard the aircraft. Lambkin's friends, including the new kid, who she had spoken with just a day before, settled into their positions with 2265 nautical miles and the unthinkable ahead of them.

The events of that awful day are history now. As I sat on my couch at 9:03 a.m., watching the North Tower of the World Trade Center burn, I saw United 175, the flight that Lambkin could easily have been on, and the flight that the new kid, the one she had spoken to the day before, *was on*, disintegrate into the South Tower, and into a billion pieces of forever lost lives, hopes and dreams.

En route to Chicago, Lambkin's plane, like all the others, was diverted and landed as quickly and safely as possible. Her plane was diverted to an airport in Canada and a couple of days later her crew commuted to Philadelphia. A day or two later, she caught a train back to Boston. As her train passed New York City, she could still see the smoke in the air from the collapsed towers and she couldn't shake the memory of the friends and co-workers she had lost only days before. She still can't. She doesn't want to.

She has told me in the time since that day of dozens of stories that she has heard from fellow flight attendants, including her roommate from training, and pilots who could have been on that flight, but for whatever reason, were not. There are hundreds of stories around America now, about people who could or should have been on any one of the flights that were taken that day, but were not.

A lot of people died that day. Far too many. But ironically, a lot of people were born on that day as well. Lambkin was one of them. September 11th wasn't listed on her birth certificate, but it was her birthday just the same.

I asked her one time if she had always been the free spirit that she is now. I don't know her any other way. A young woman given to spirituality, yin and yang, following her heart and pursuing happiness with reckless abandon. She told me that she hadn't, but that it changed on 9/11/01.

She learned that day, in a very real, all too painful way, how precious life is and how quickly and randomly it can be taken. She began, that very day, to divest herself of the weights of the world that bogged her down. The same weights and distractions that bog so many of us down. While she was on furlough from the airline, she used her travel benefit to see the world. She visited places that Arkansas farm girls don't often visit. She experienced life fully, and she enjoyed every minute of it. She still does. She lives for the moment and finds joy in everything she does. She told me once, "When drinking from the cup of life – CHUG!!" She still, 14 years later, proudly serves as a flight attendant for United Airlines.

She makes sure that she's working every September 11th, partly as a tribute to her fallen comrades and partly in defiance of the events that did so much to steal away the happiness of so many.

So today, on this September 11th, I want to wish my sweet Lambkin a happy birthday. A young woman, born in her thirties, on September 11, 2001.

About the Author

▼◄ ▲ ▼◄ ▲ ▼◄ ▲ ▼◄ ▲ ▼◄ ▲ ▼◄ ▲ ▼◄ ▲ ▼◄ ▲

With Irish roots and a childhood in Northern Colorado, Tim Shea is an All American kind of guy. His work ethic and curiosity about the world lead him into fascinating and heartfelt encounters with people from all walks of life. Tim apprenticed in the fine art of storytelling with his father, his Uncle Don, and his own practice of truly listening when people talk. He lives in Boston with his sons.

Made in the USA
San Bernardino, CA
06 November 2015